JUMBO
BORDERS BOOK

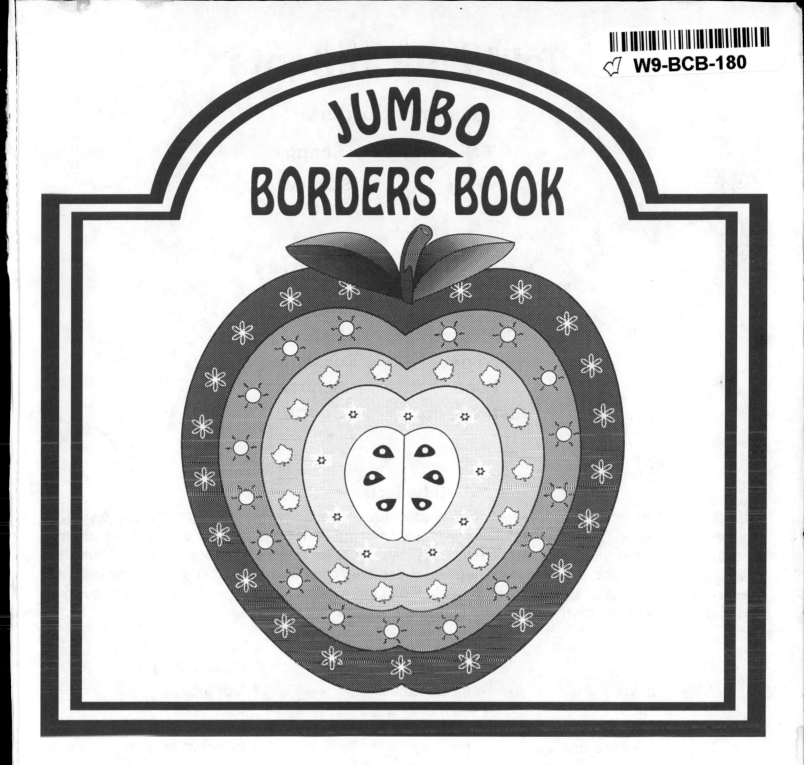

Teacher Created Materials, Inc.
P.O. Box 1040
Huntington Beach, CA 92647
©*1997 Teacher Created Materials, Inc.*
ISBN-1-57690-092-4
Made in U.S.A.

Illustrated by
TCM Art Staff

Cover Art by
Darlene Spivak

Table of Contents

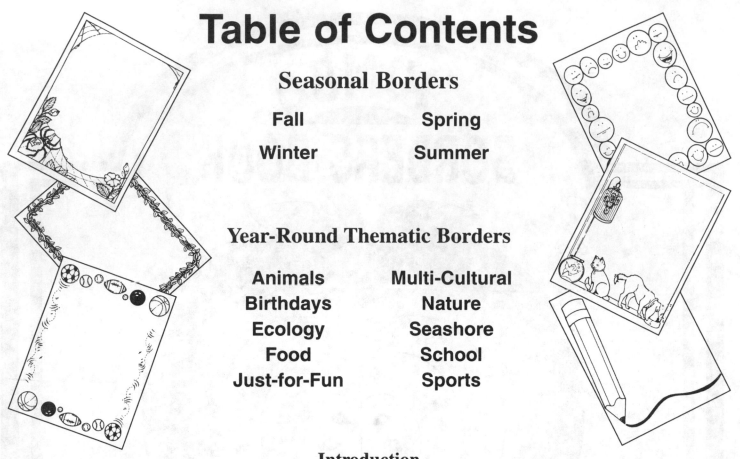

Seasonal Borders

Year-Round Thematic Borders

Introduction

The *Jumbo Borders Book* is a collection of borders for seasons, and themes throughout the year. Designed for the busy teacher, this book will be a welcome addition to anyone who wants to be a bit creative without the fuss. Teacher Created Materials' most exceptional borders have been collected and organized into one jumbo book. They have been conveniently arranged in two general groups—seasonal and thematic. Each border is presented in three different sizes—full page, half page, quarter page — giving you many choices for use. Here are some suggestions.

Full Page
- stationery
- awards
- field trip notices
- conference notices
- creative writing paper
- PTA information
- flyers
- newsletters
- holiday announcements
- student journals

Half Page
- certificates
- invitations
- permission slips
- memos
- greeting cards
- notes home
- notes school
- recipe cards
- photo frames
- phone messages

Quarter Page
- labeling
- bookmarks
- game pieces
- incentive awards
- room passes
- name tags
- place cards
- pin-on reminders
- flash cards for math, spelling, language

"How-To" Assembly Hints

After you have chosen a border, make a copy of it so you do not need to cut the book apart. On the copy, write, type, or paste any text you wish to appear inside the border. Now you are ready to make final copies of the page.

#2092 Jumbo Borders Book

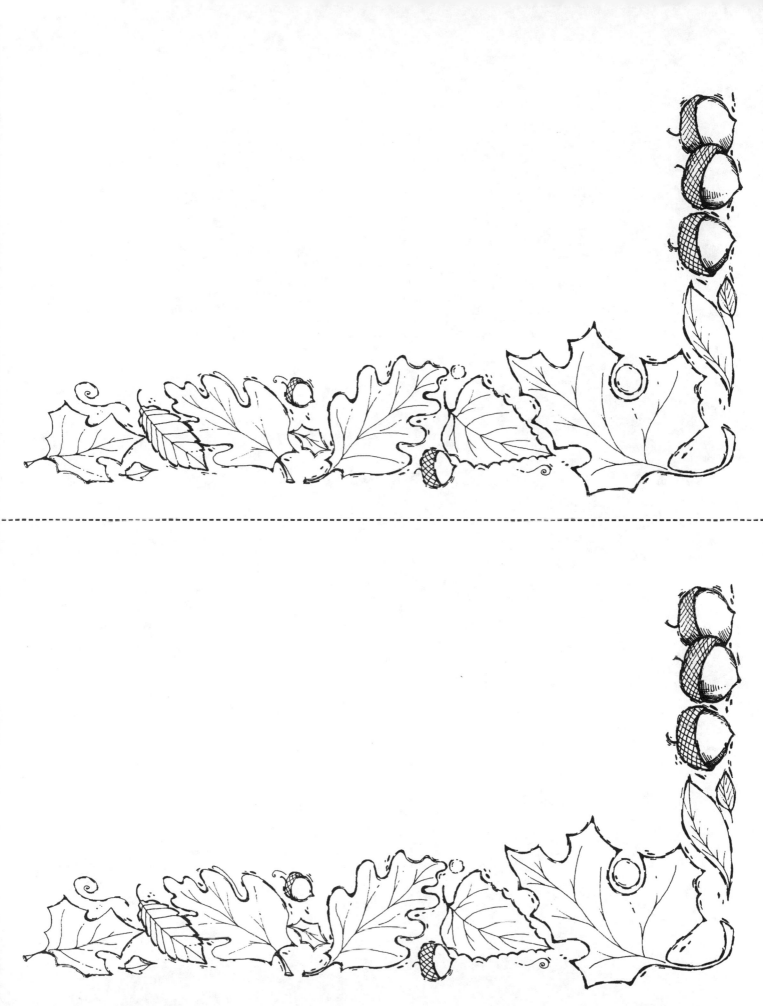

#2092 Jumbo Borders Book

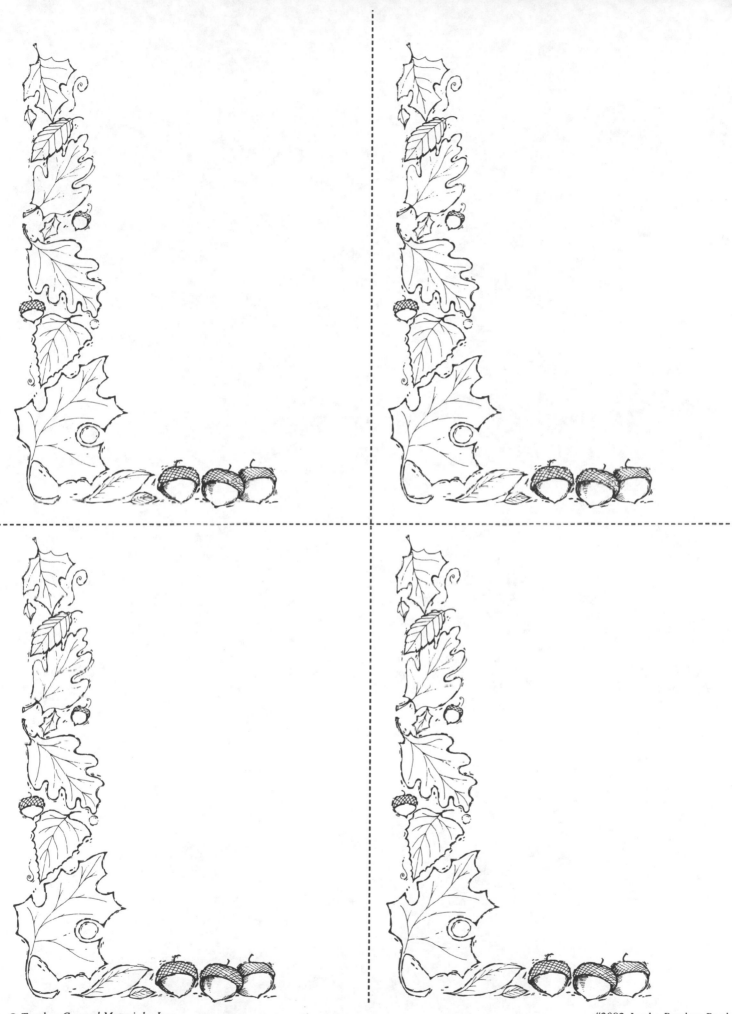

#2092 Jumbo Borders Book

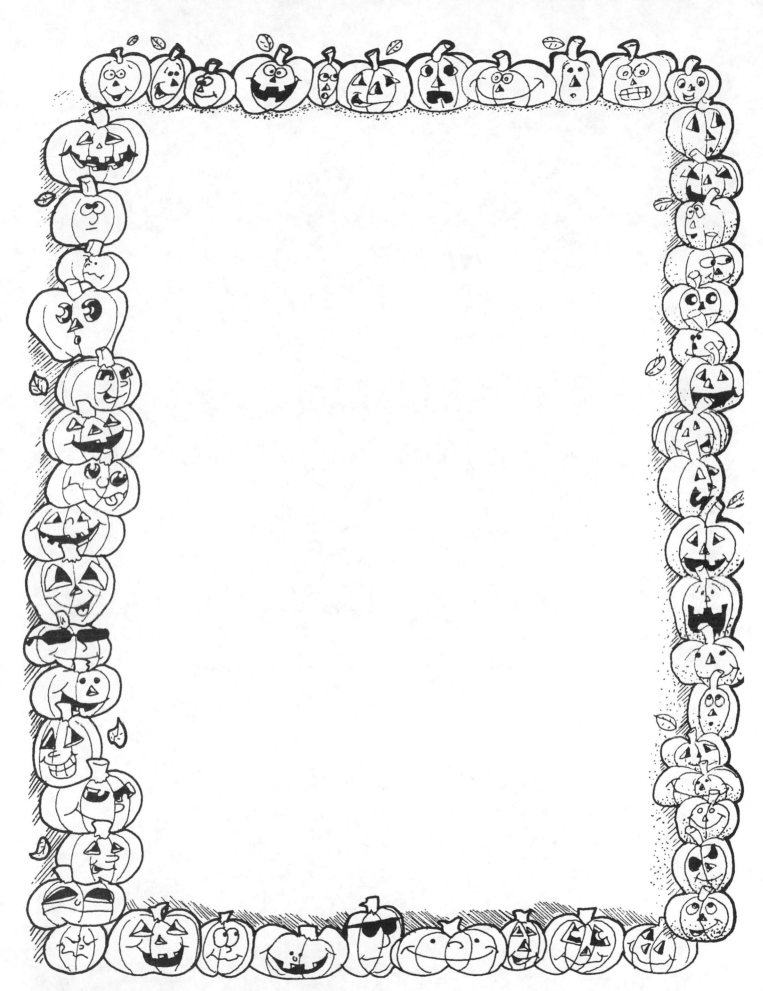

#2092 Jumbo Borders Book

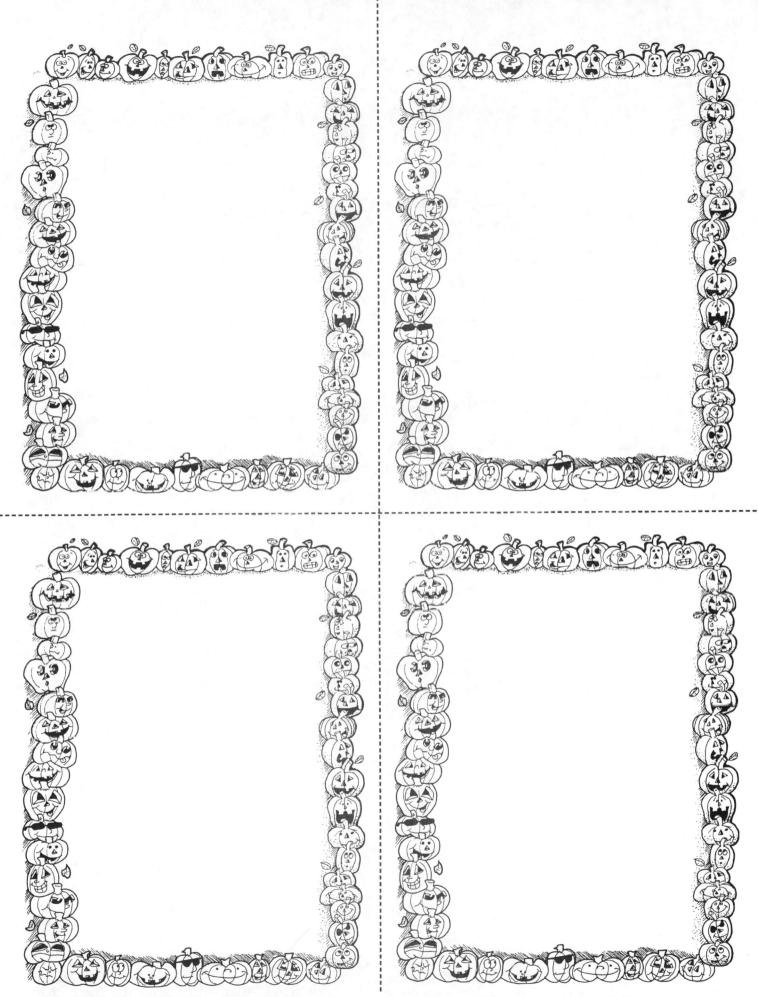

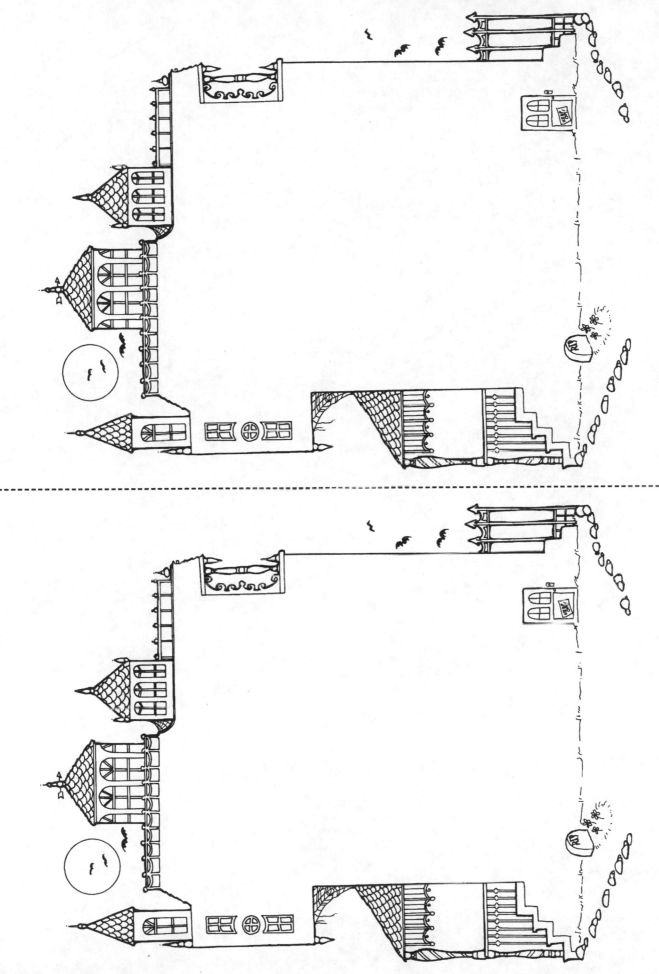

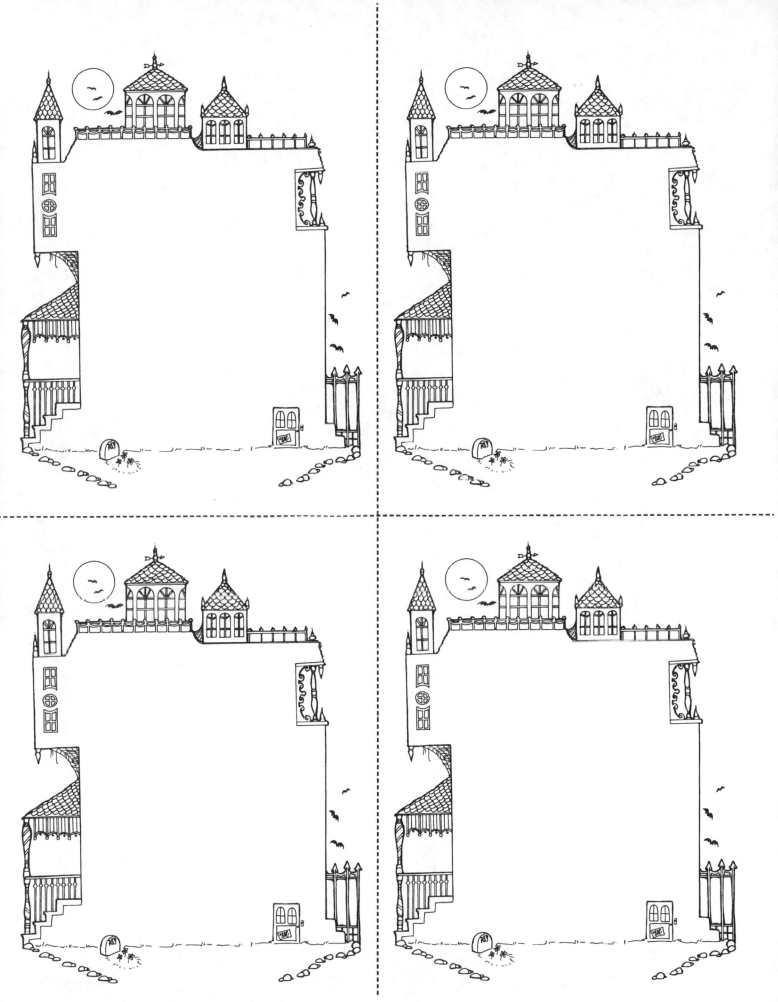

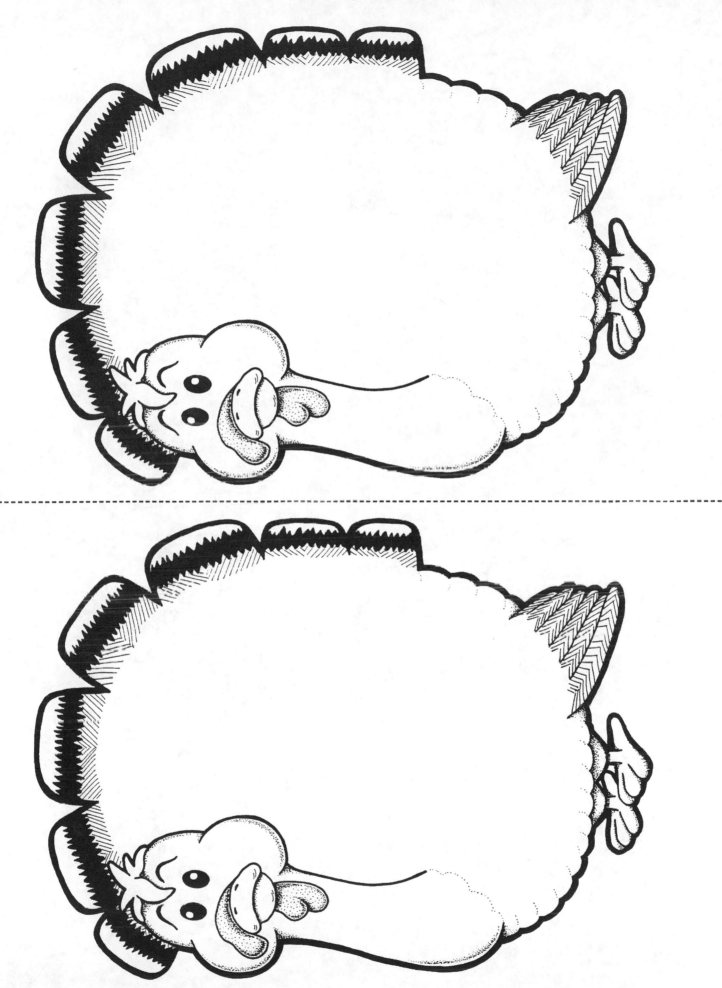

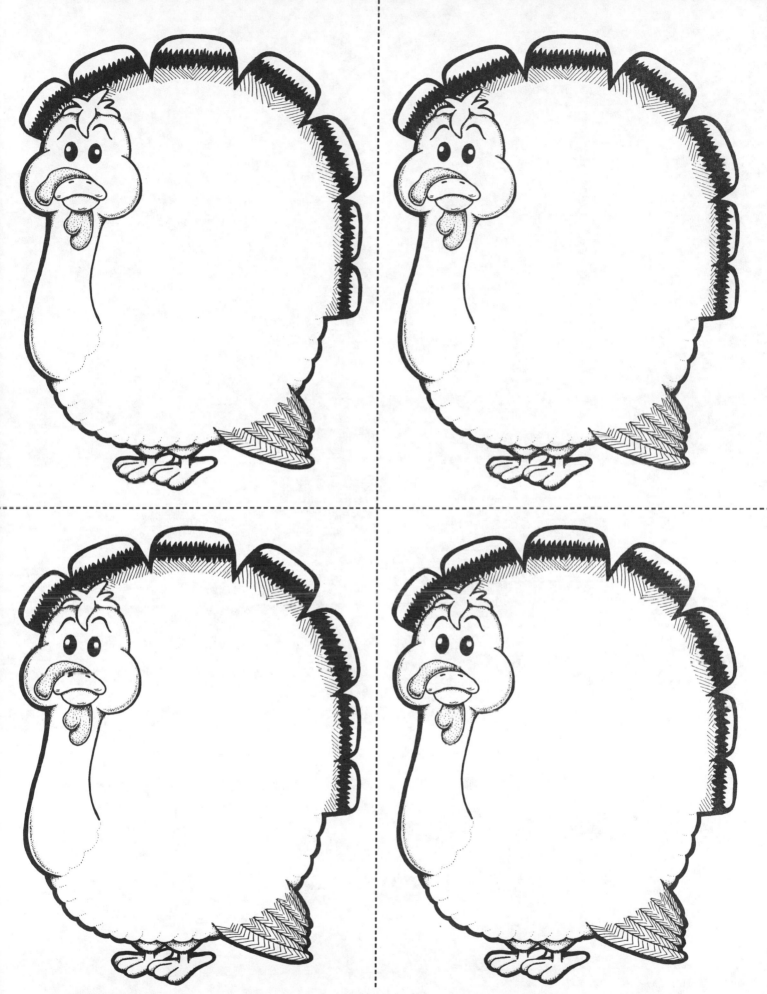

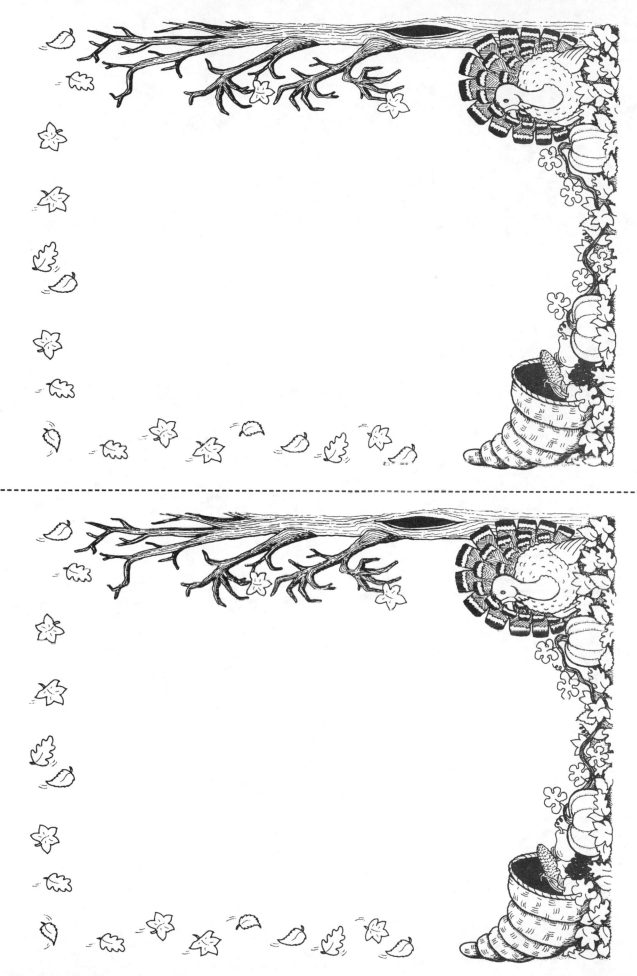

#2092 Jumbo Borders Book

#2092 Jumbo Borders Book

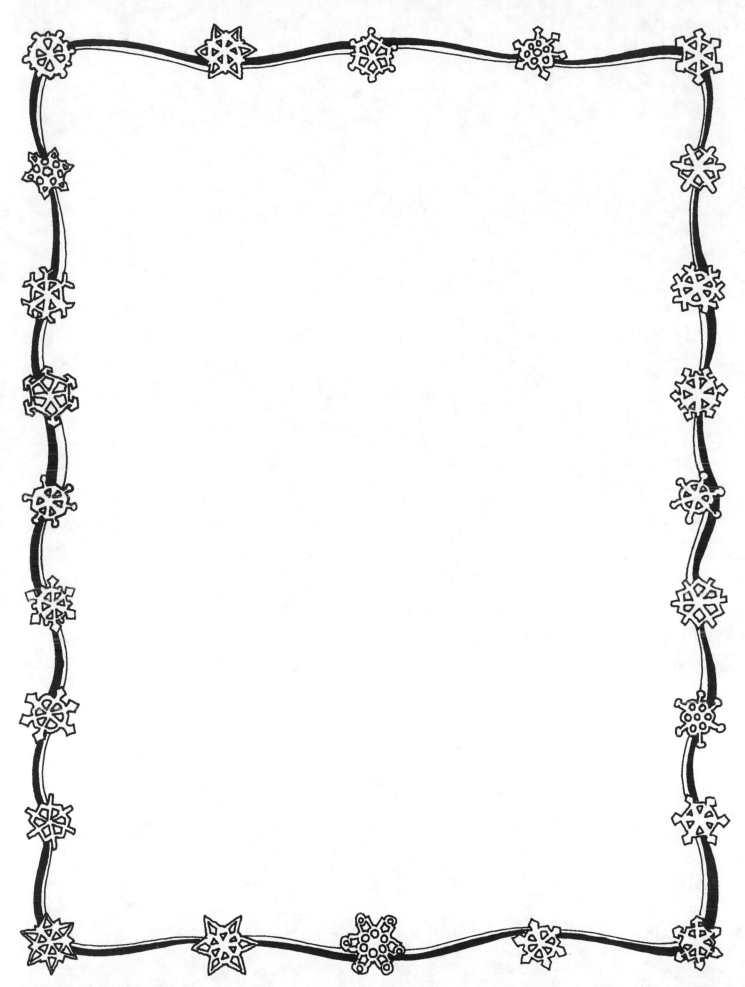

#2092 Jumbo Borders Book

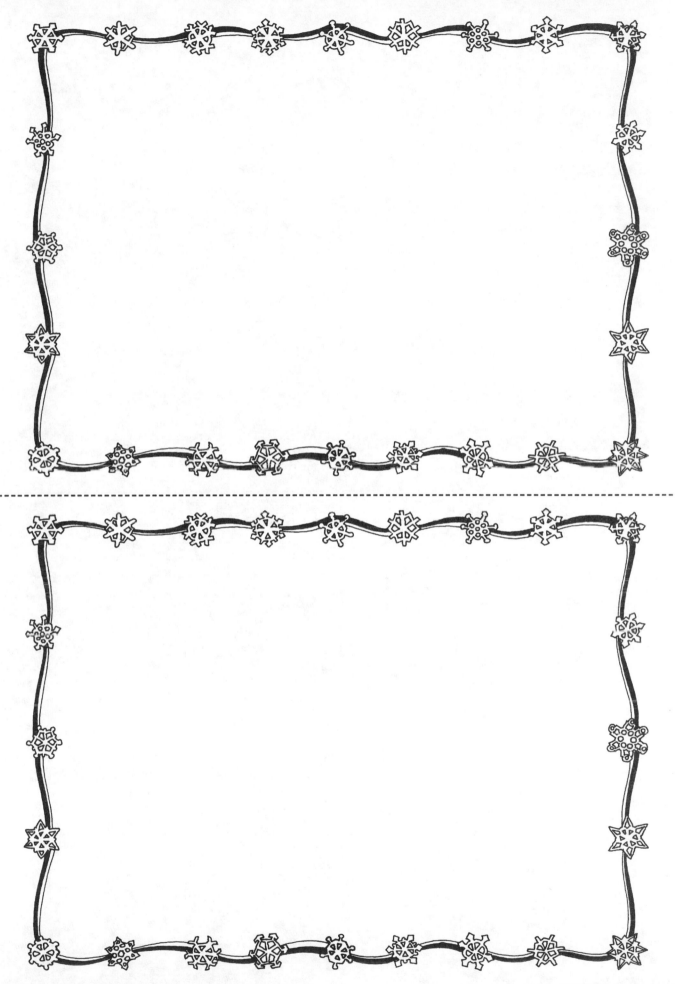

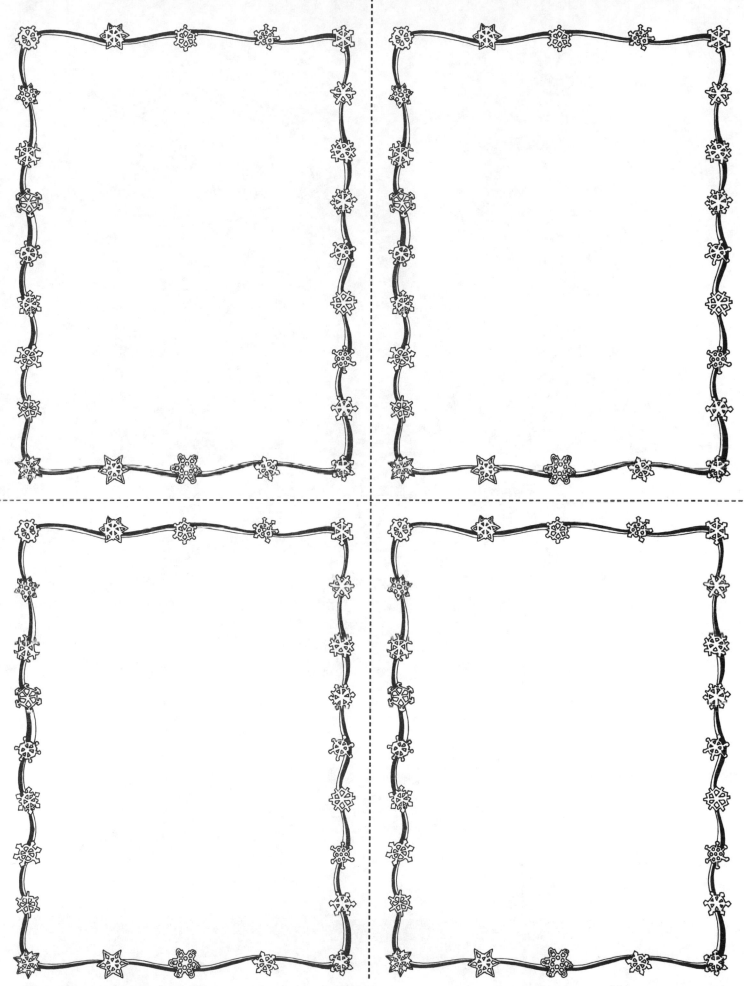

© Teacher Created Materials, Inc.

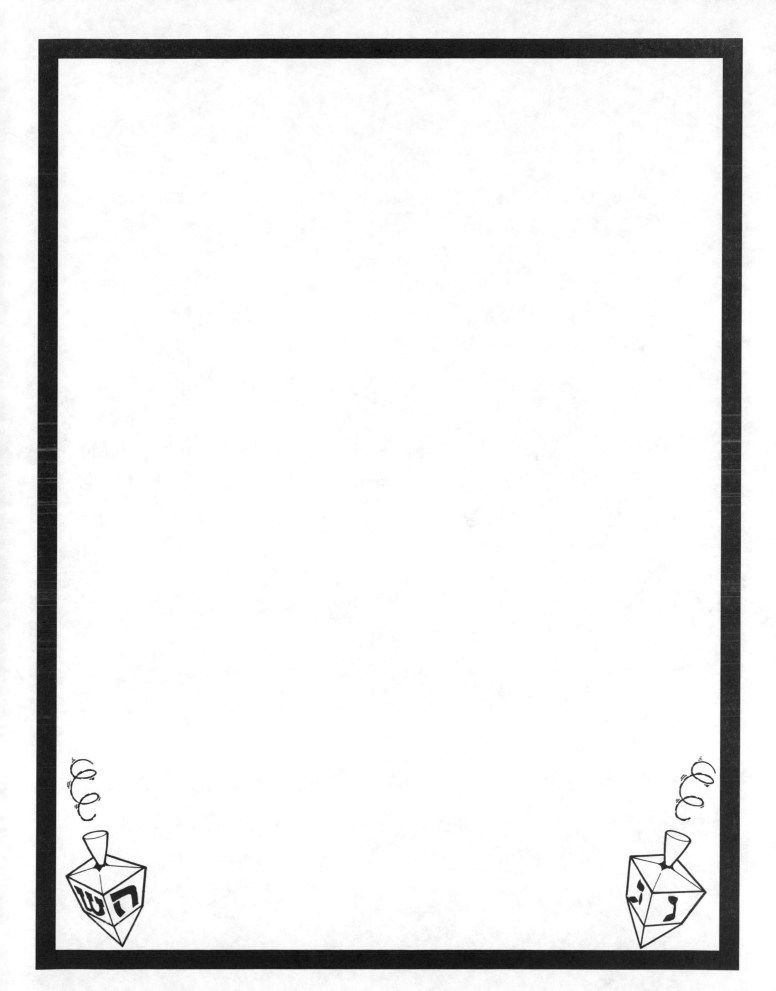

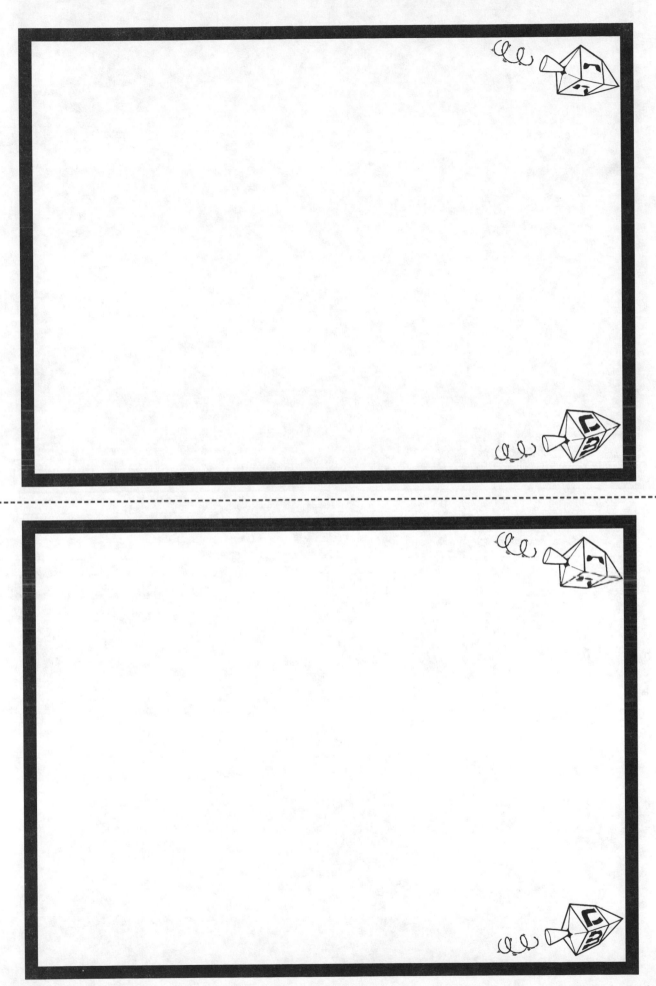

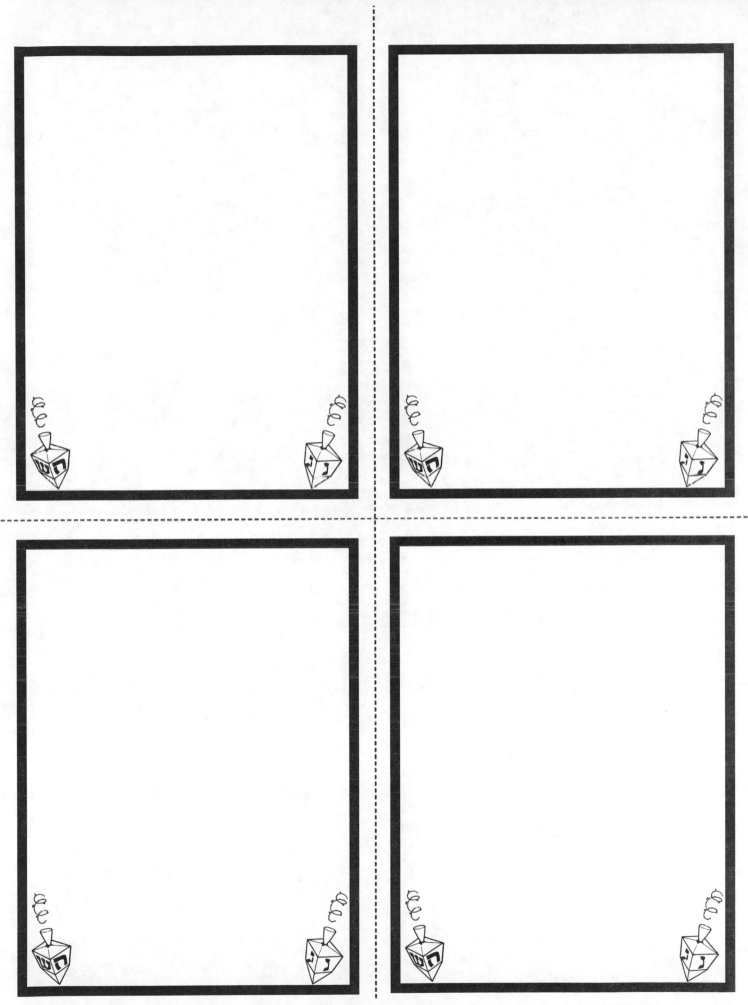

#2092 Jumbo Borders Book

© Teacher Created Materials, Inc.

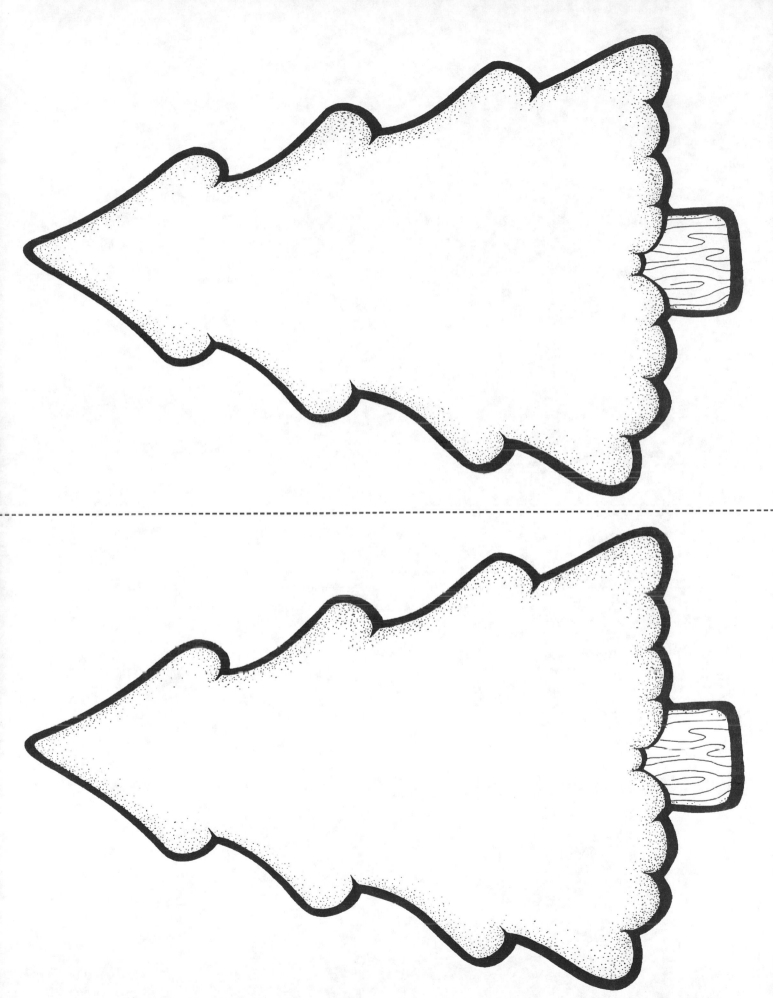

© Teacher Created Materials, Inc.

#2092 Jumbo Borders Book

#2092 Jumbo Borders Book

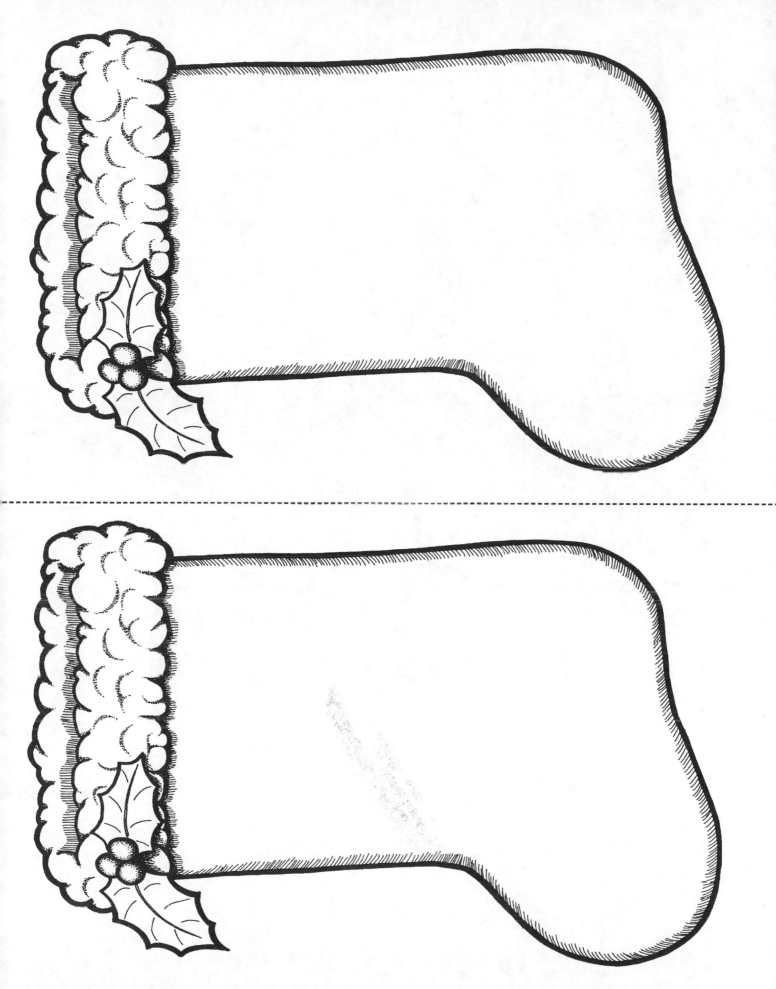

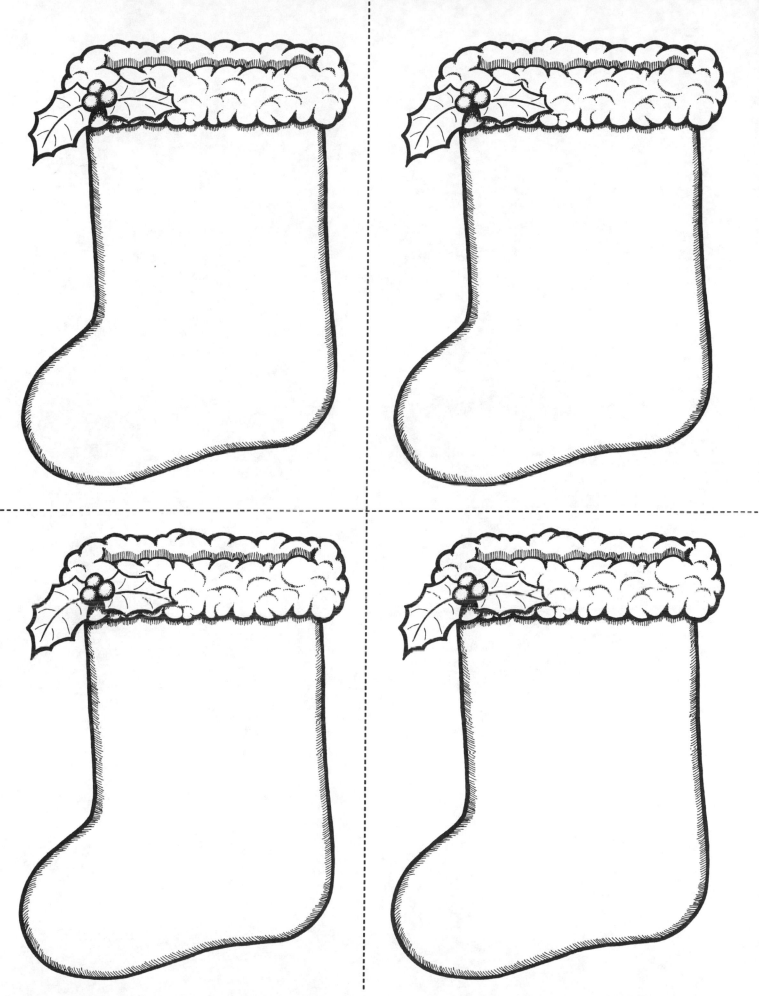

© Teacher Created Materials, Inc.

#2092 Jumbo Borders Book

#2092 Jumbo Borders Book

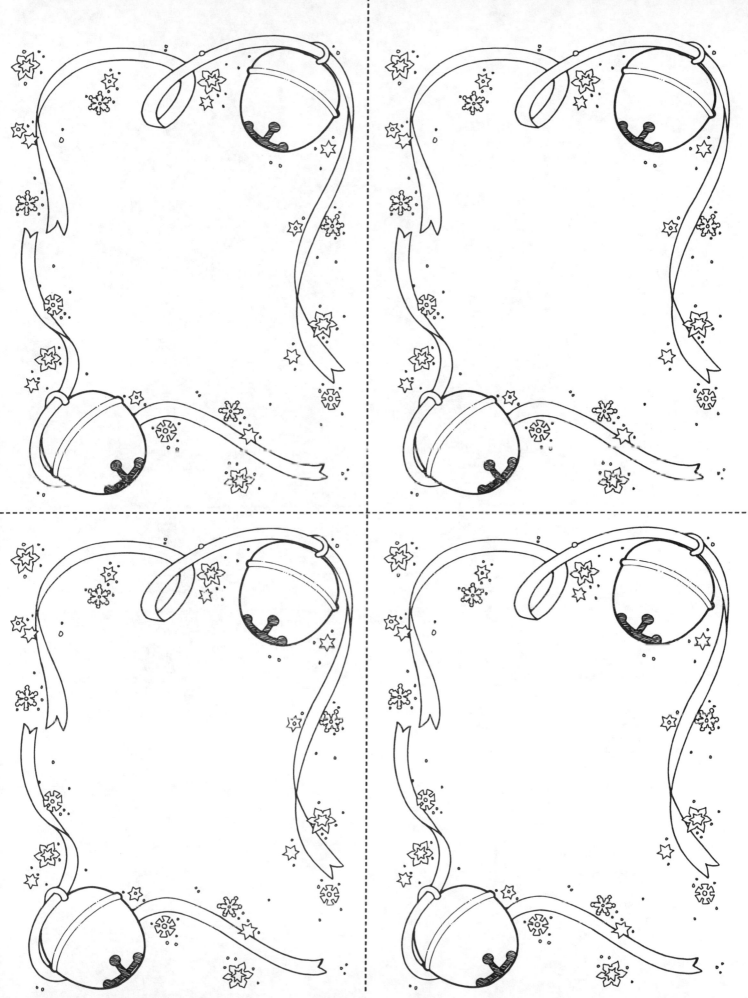

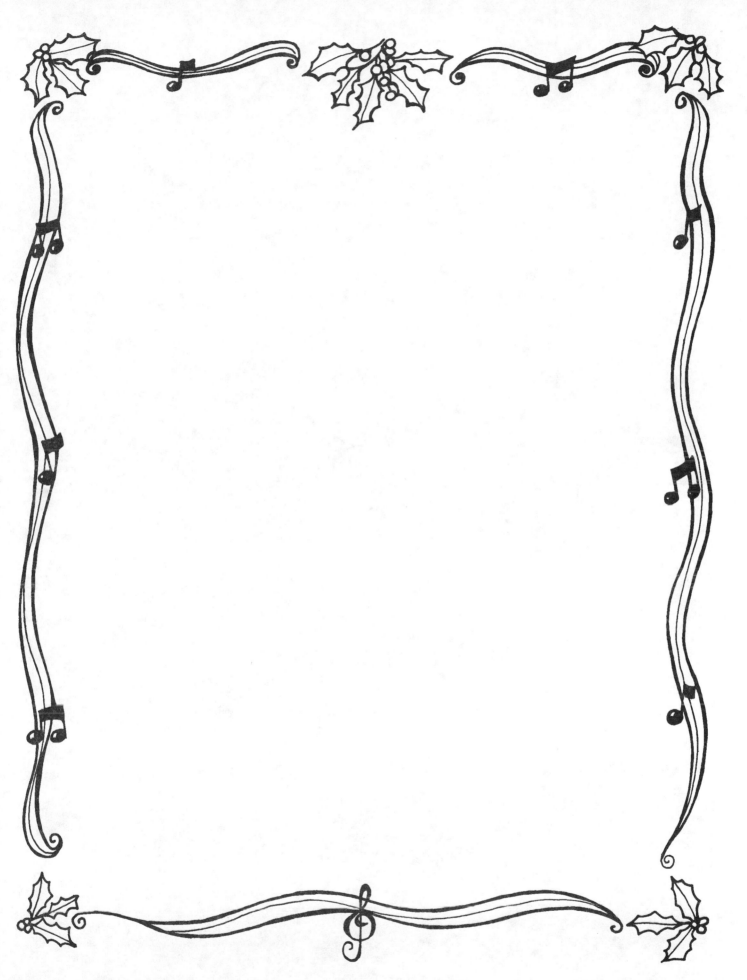

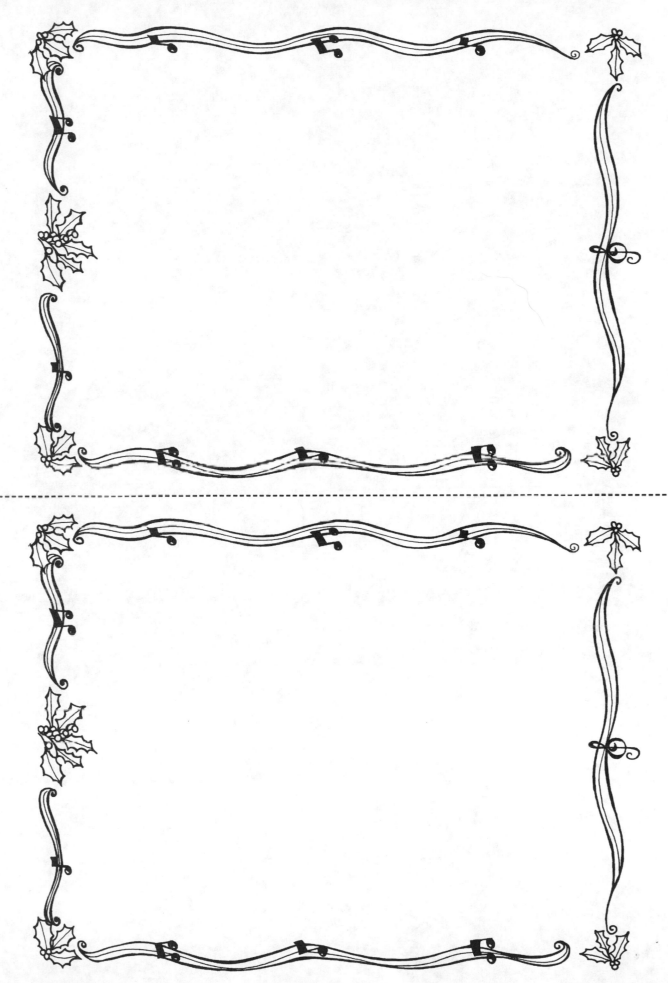

#2092 Jumbo Borders Book

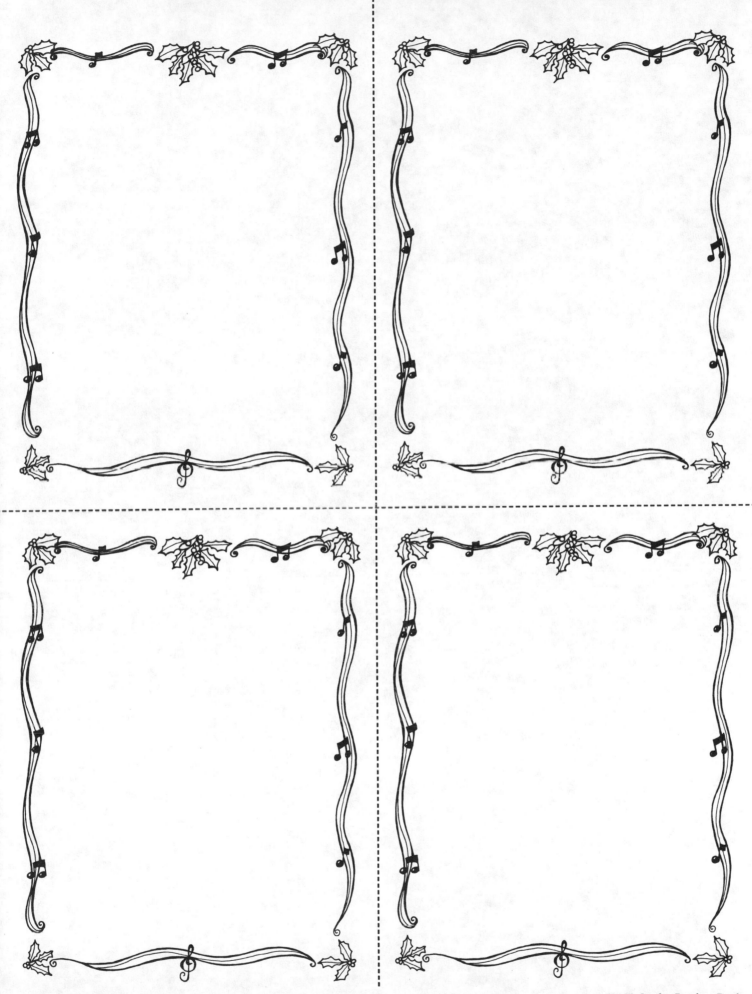

#2092 Jumbo Borders Book

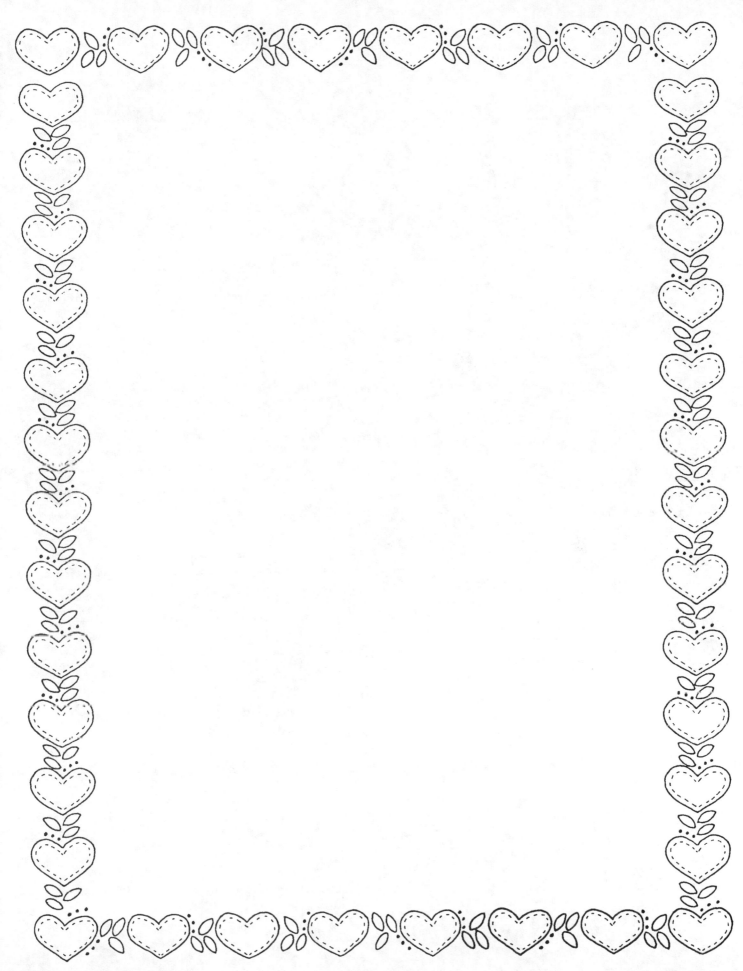

#2092 Jumbo Borders Book

#2092 Jumbo Borders Book

#2092 Jumbo Borders Book

#2092 Jumbo Borders Book

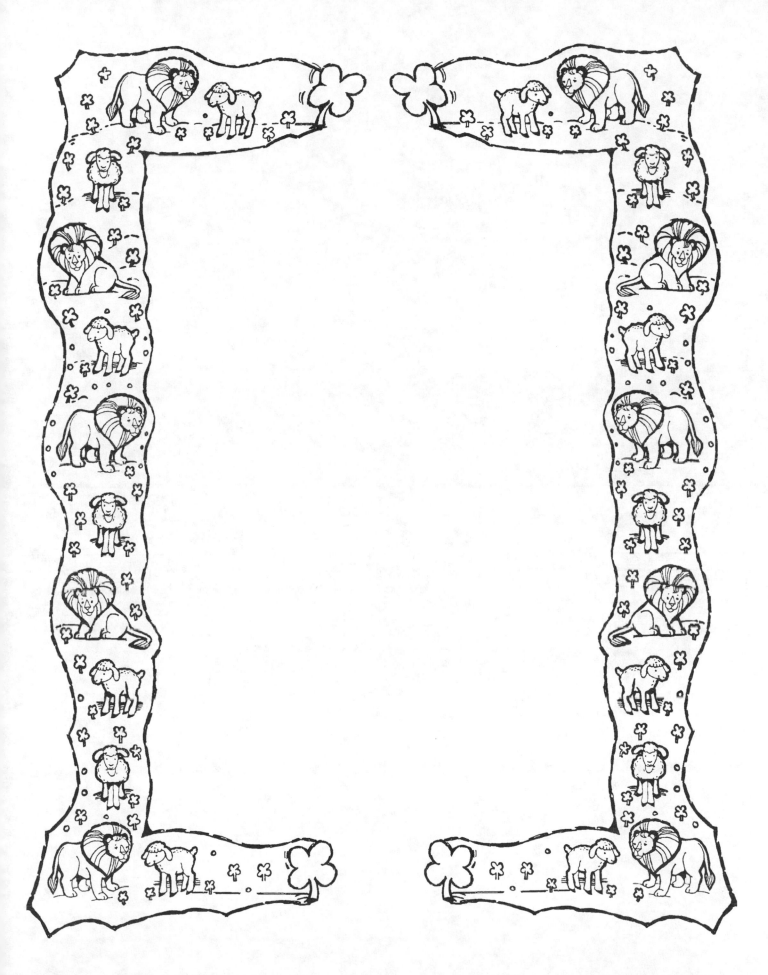

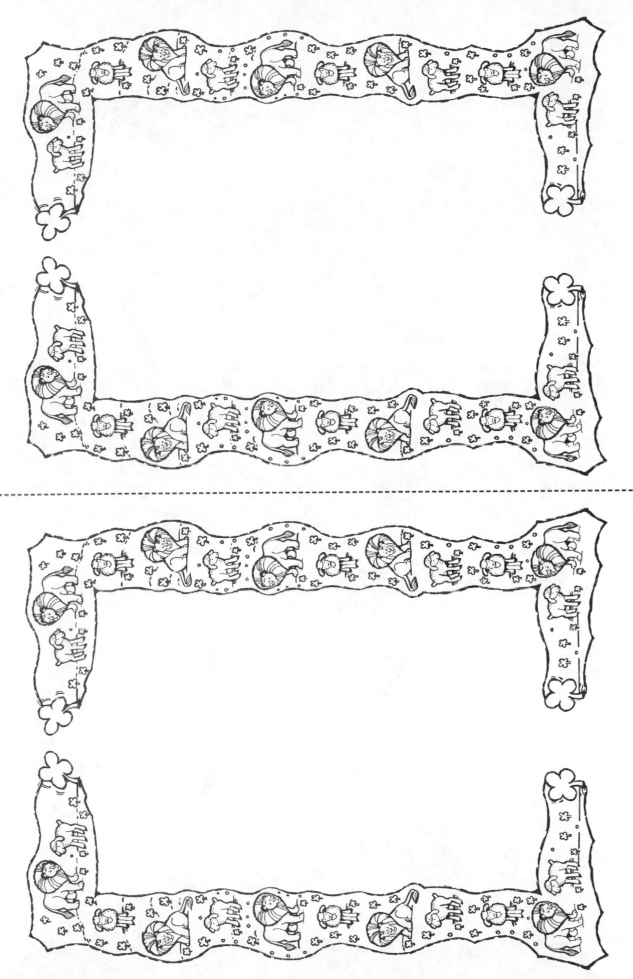

#2092 Jumbo Borders Book

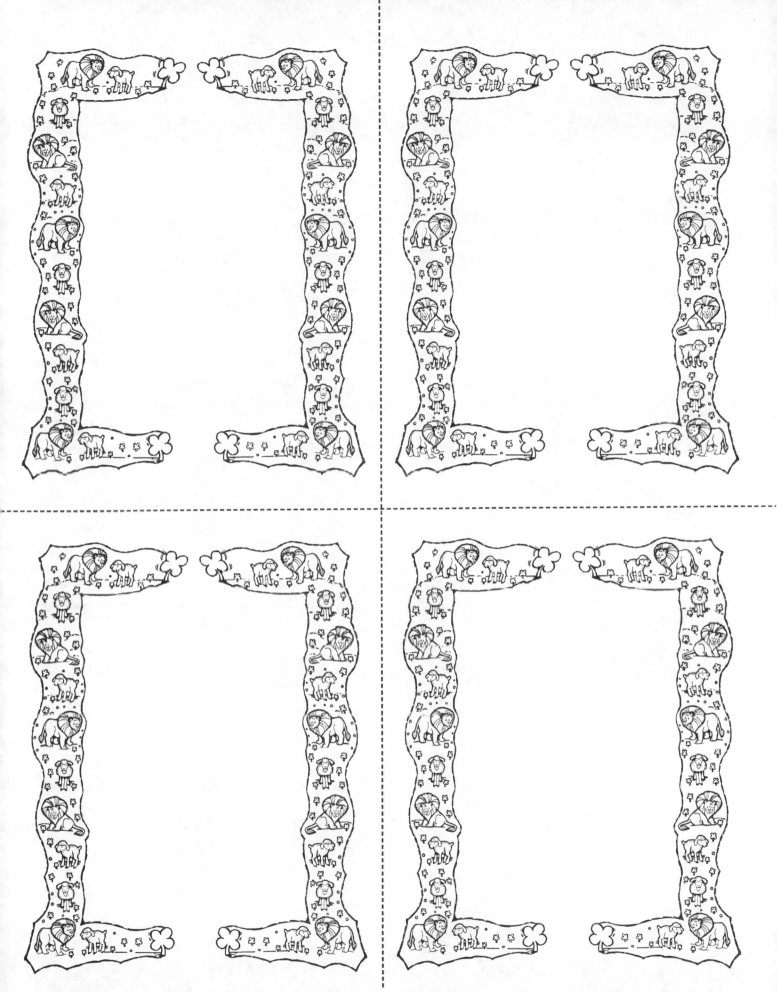

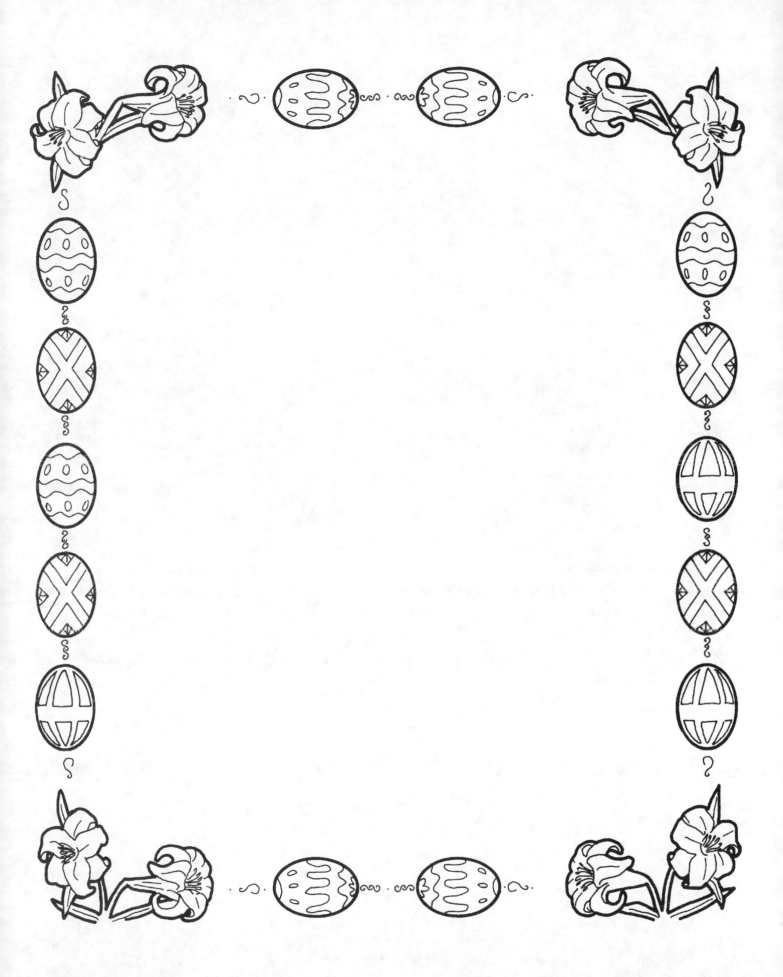

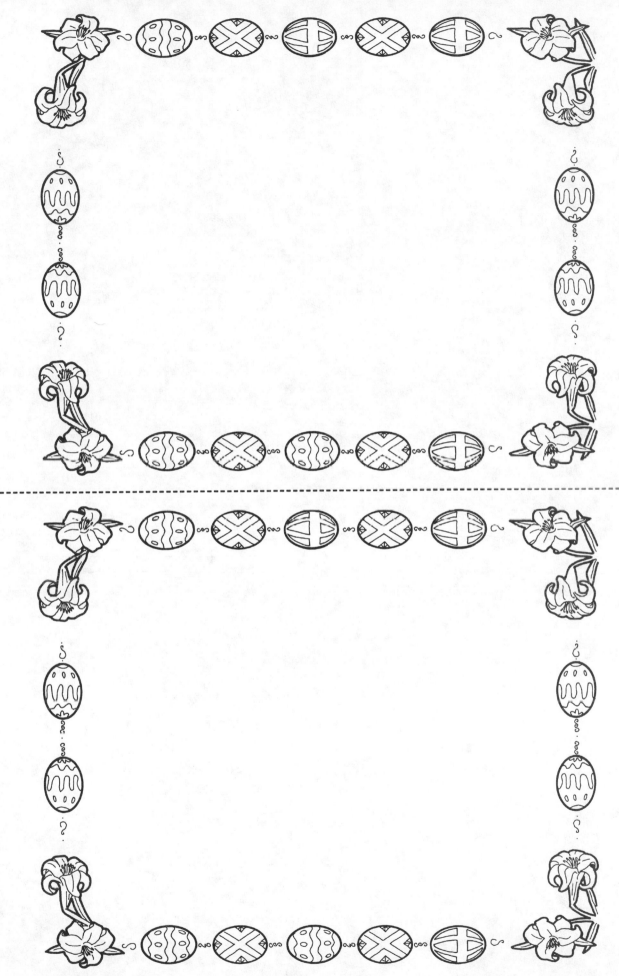

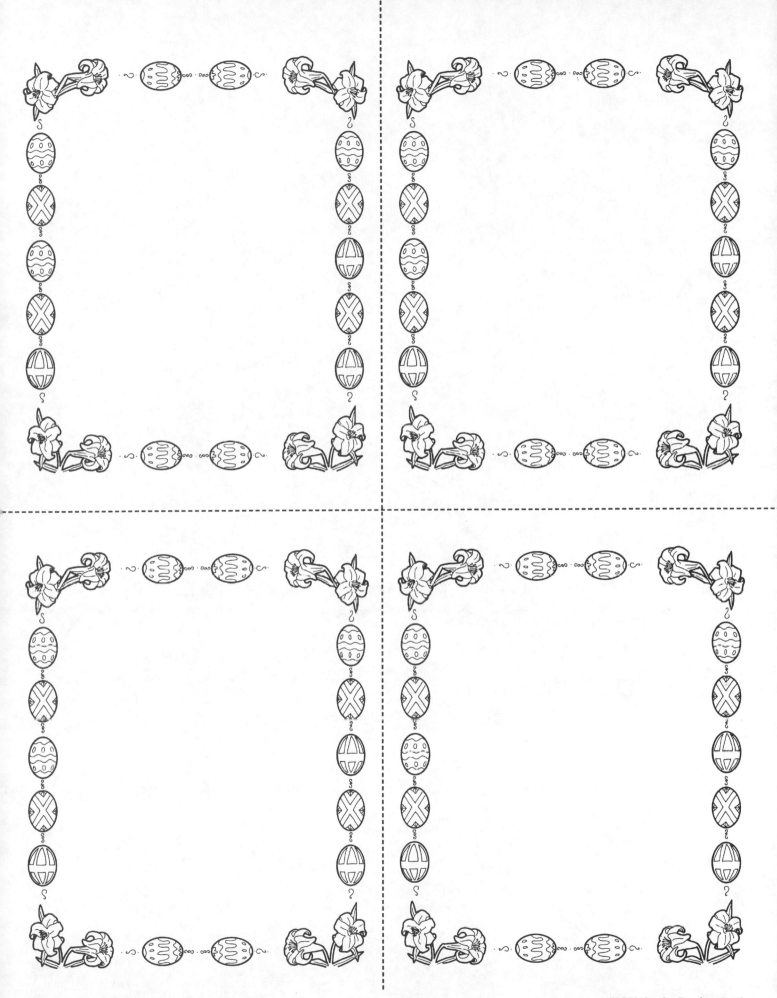

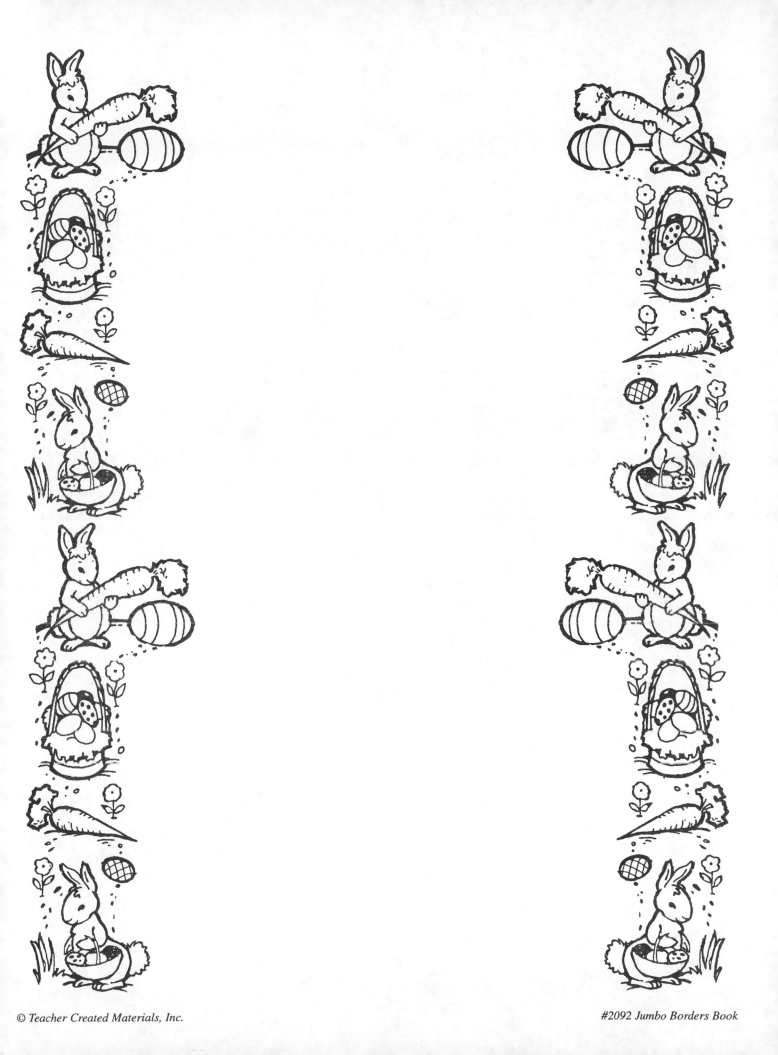

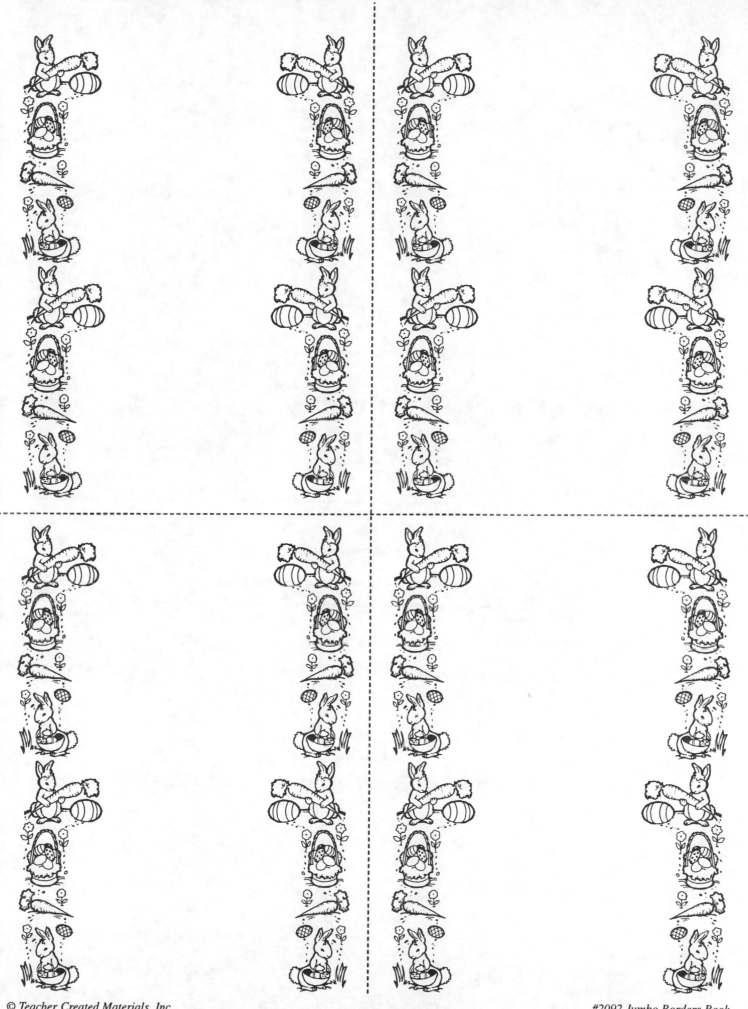

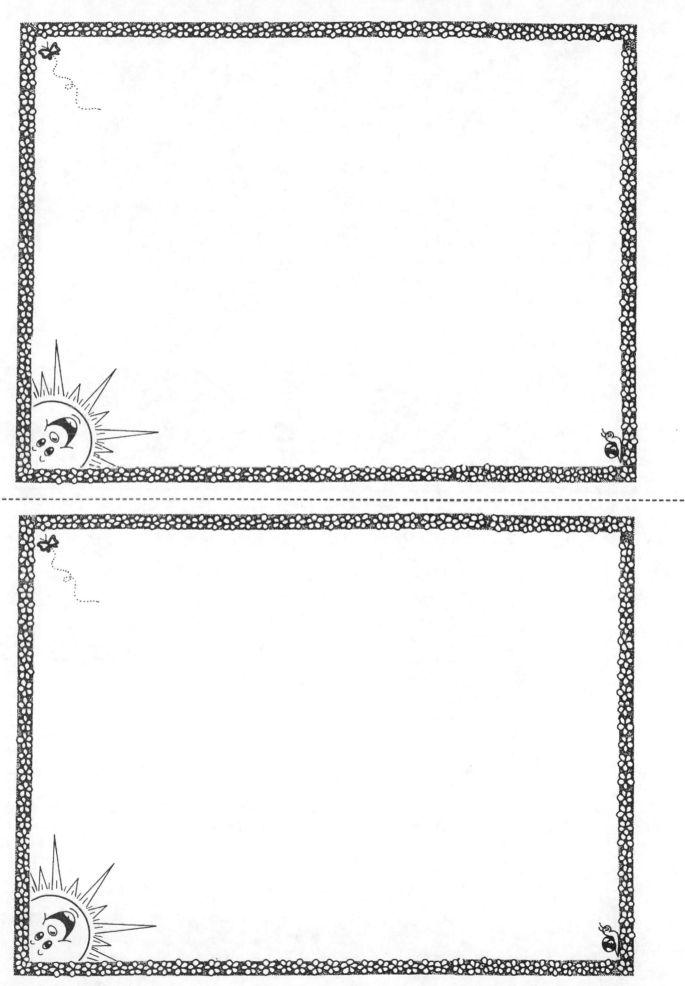

#2092 Jumbo Borders Book

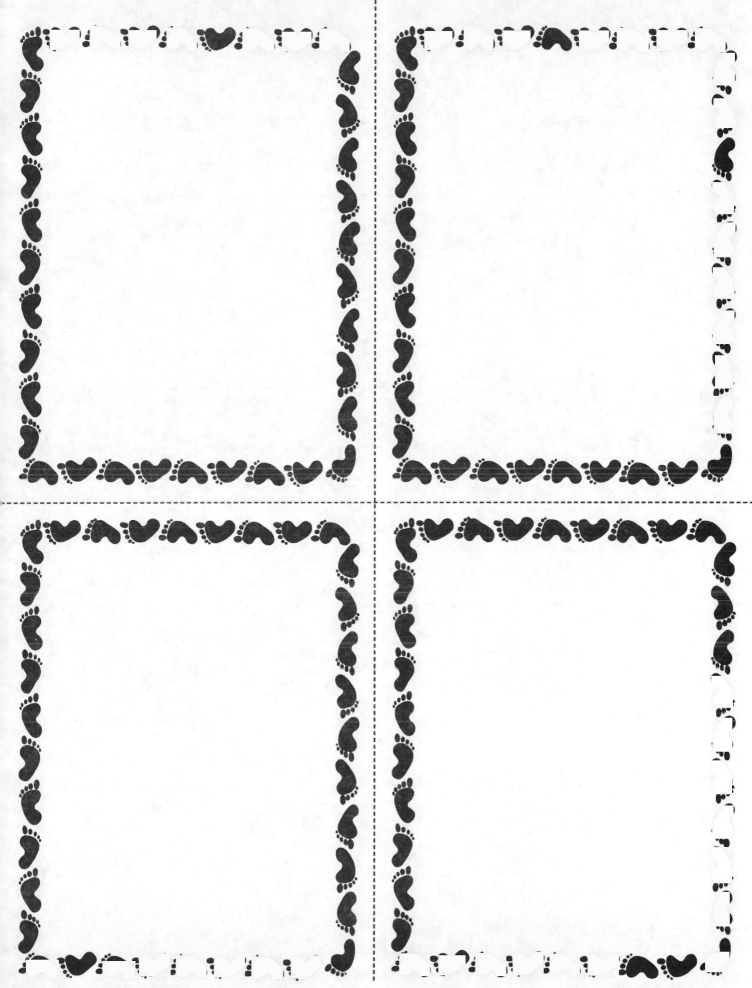

#2092 Jumbo Borders Book

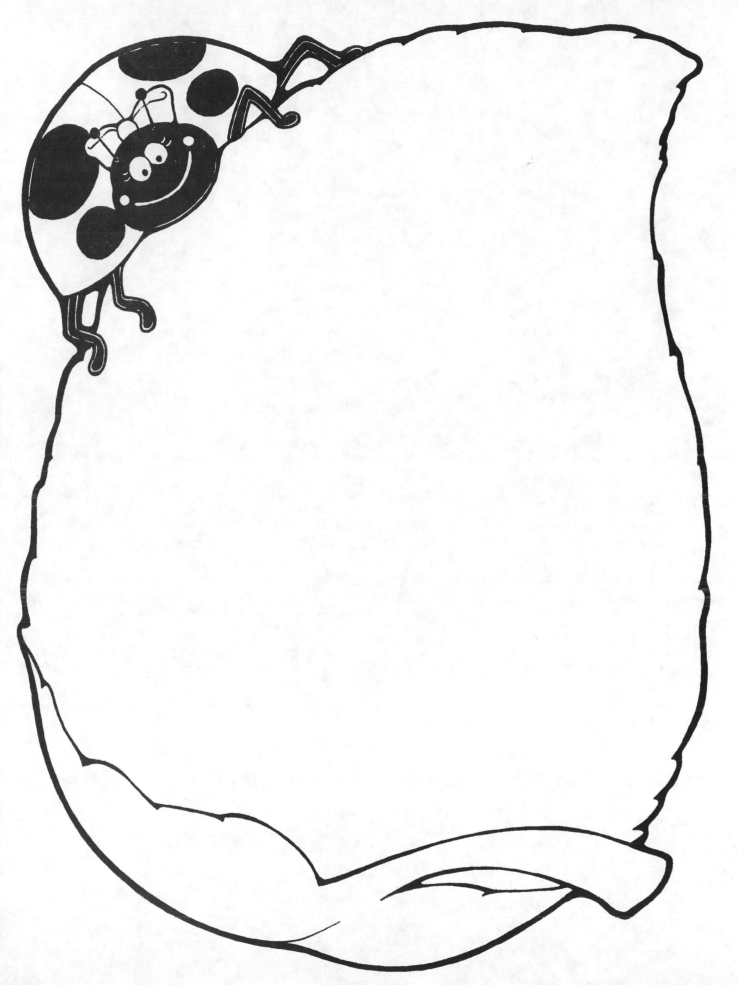

#2092 Jumbo Borders Book

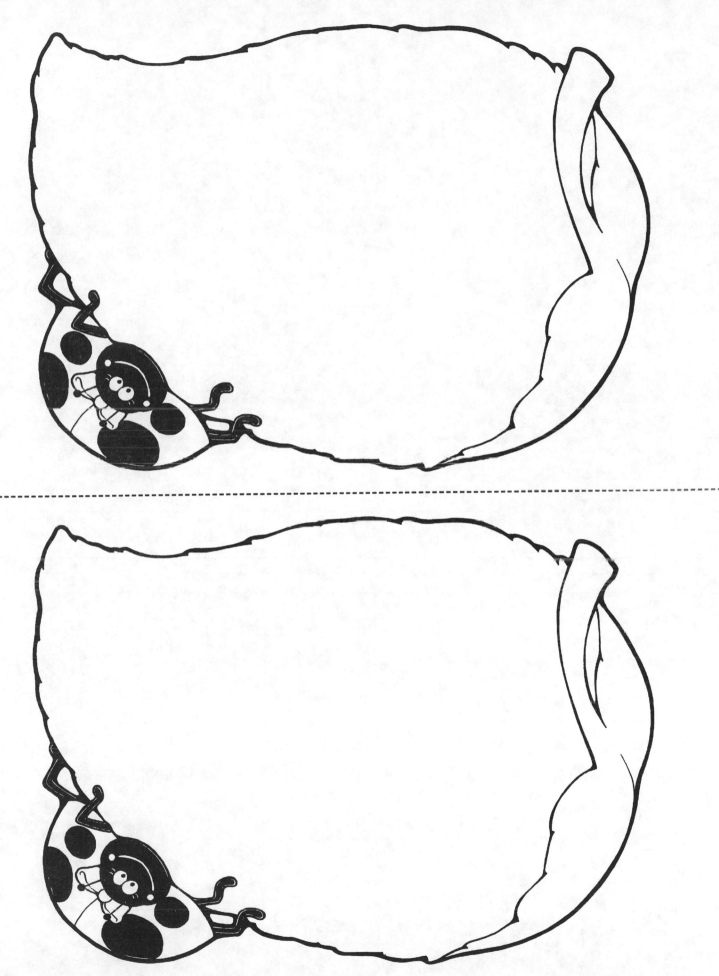

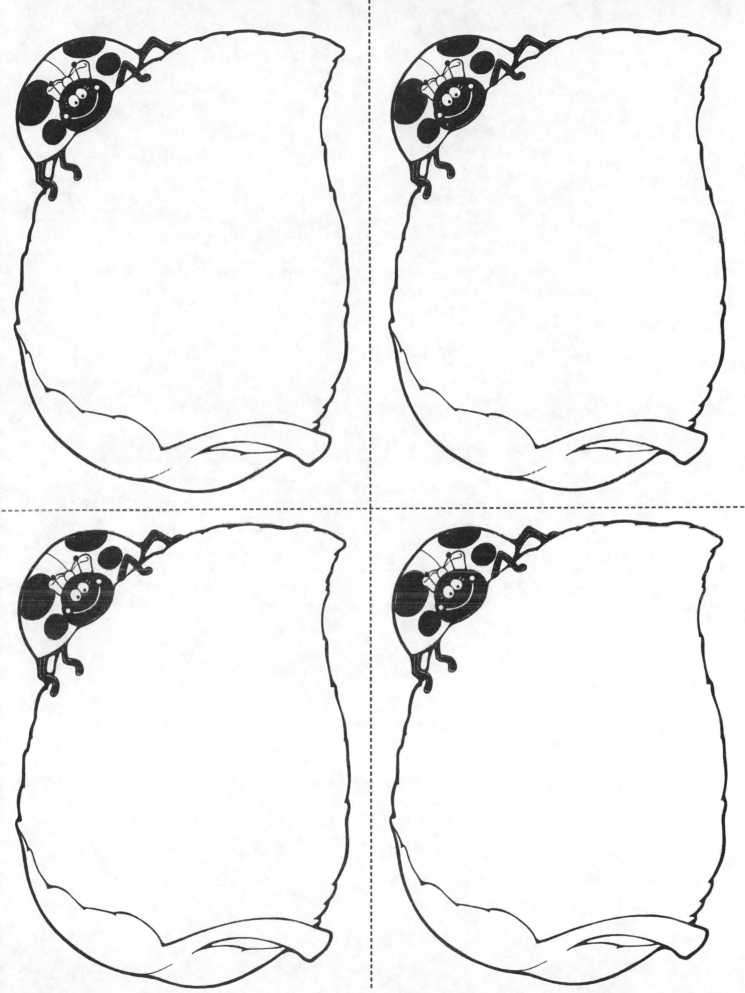

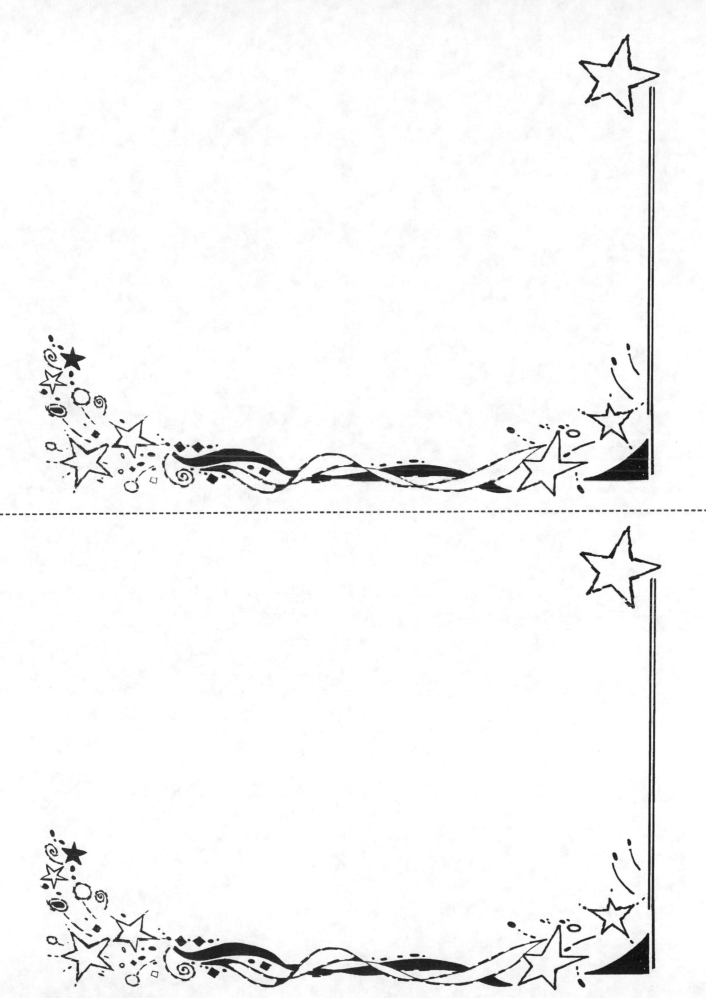

#2092 Jumbo Borders Book

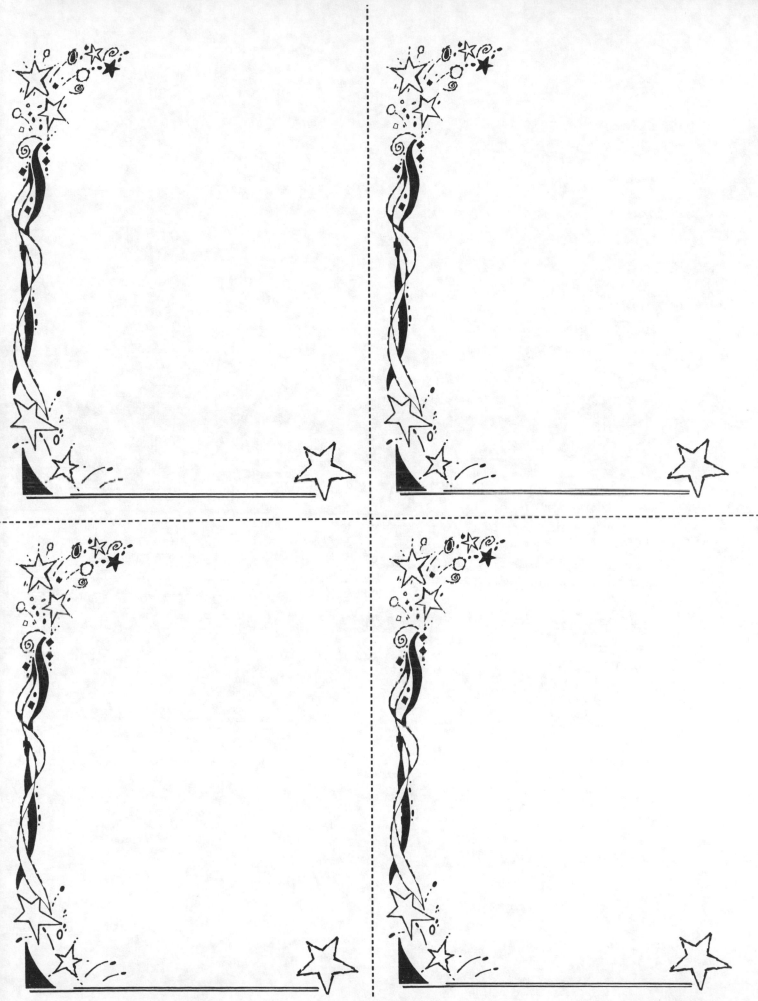

© *Teacher Created Materials, Inc.*

#2092 Jumbo Borders Book

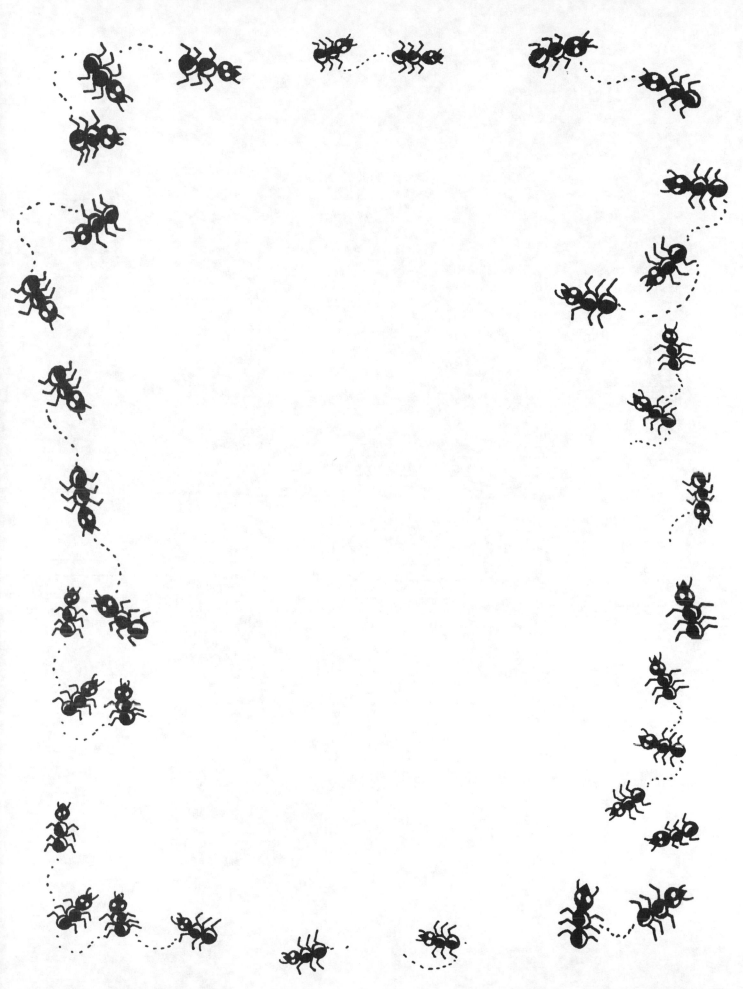

#2092 Jumbo Borders Book

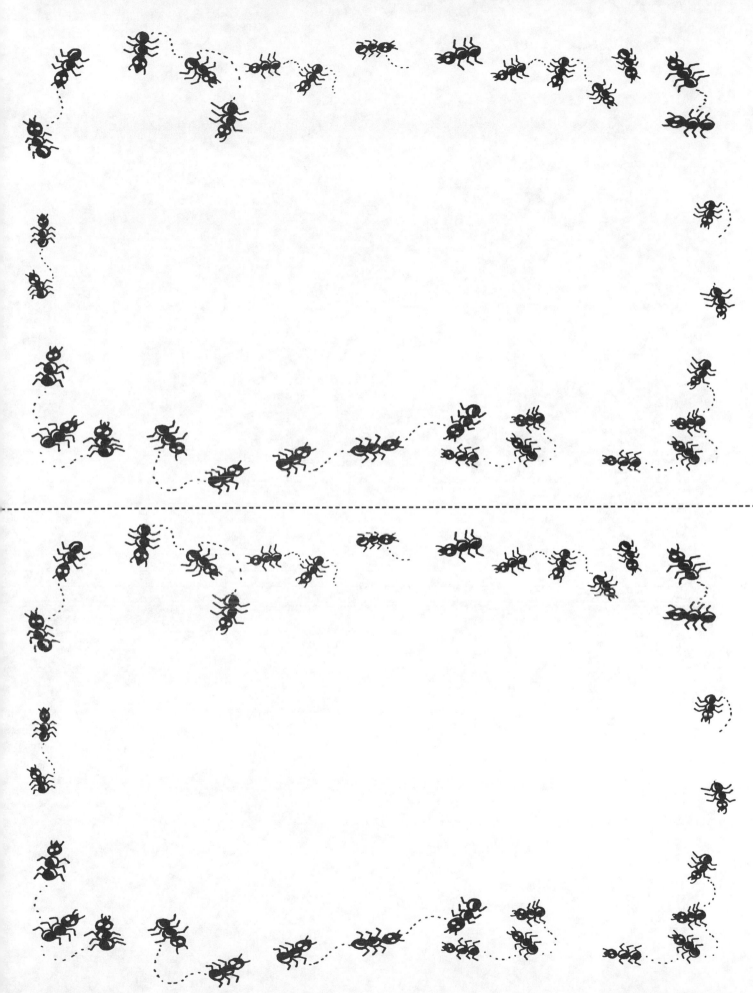

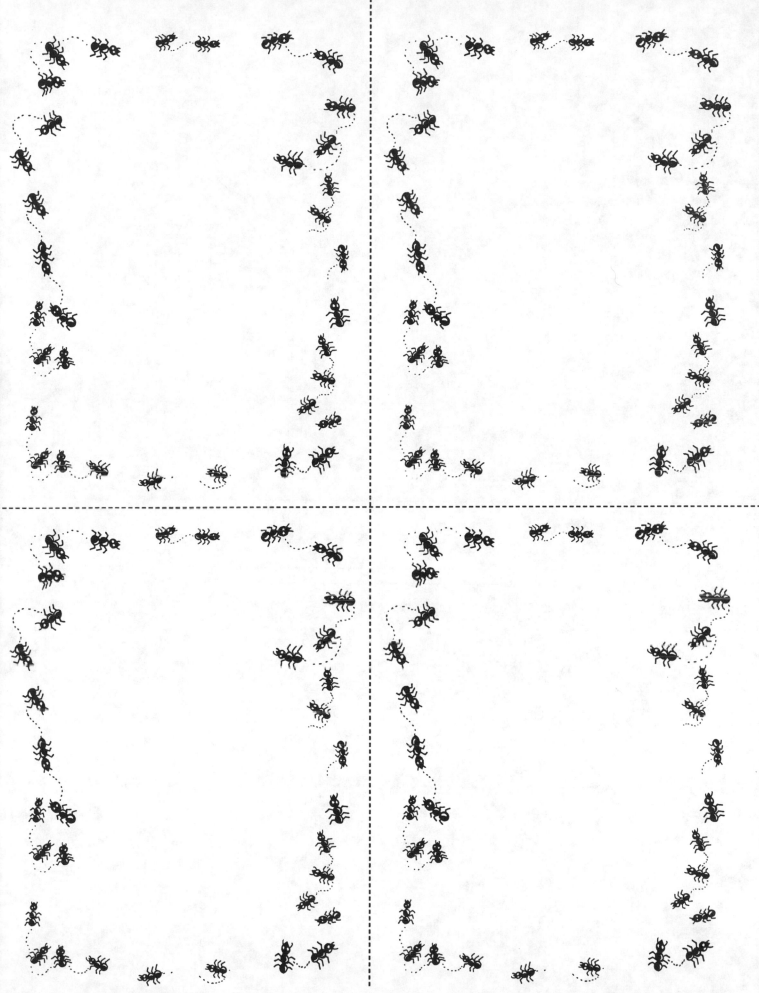

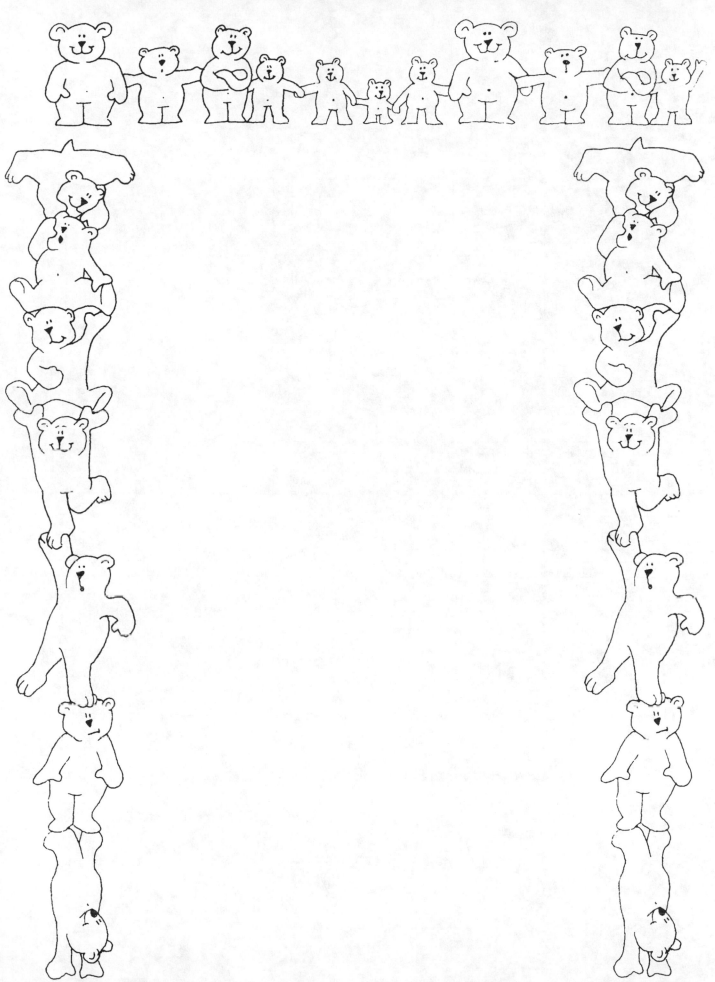

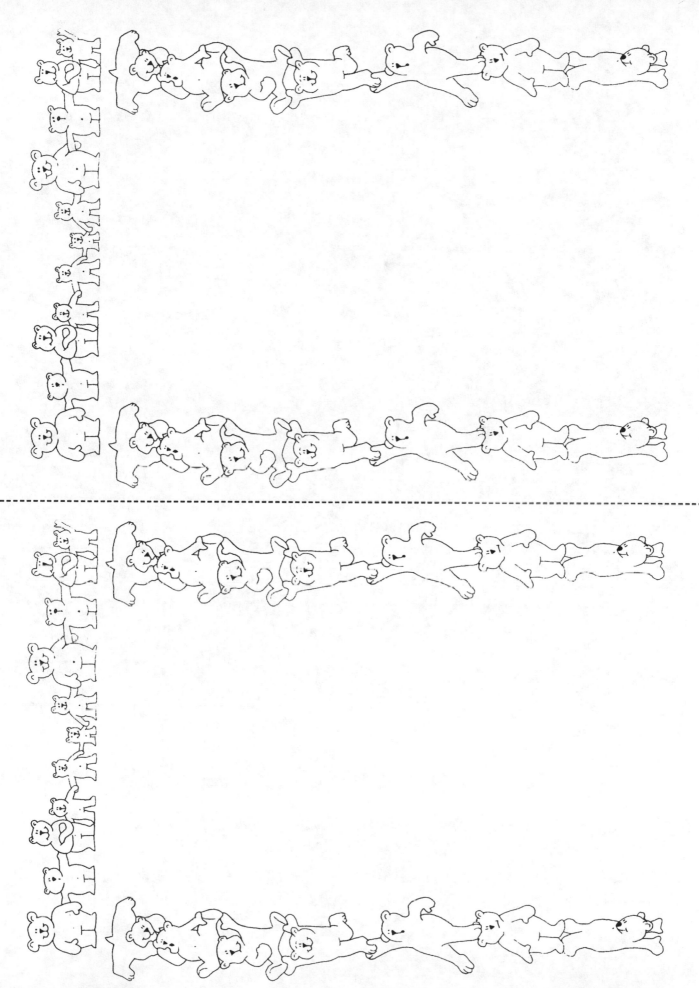

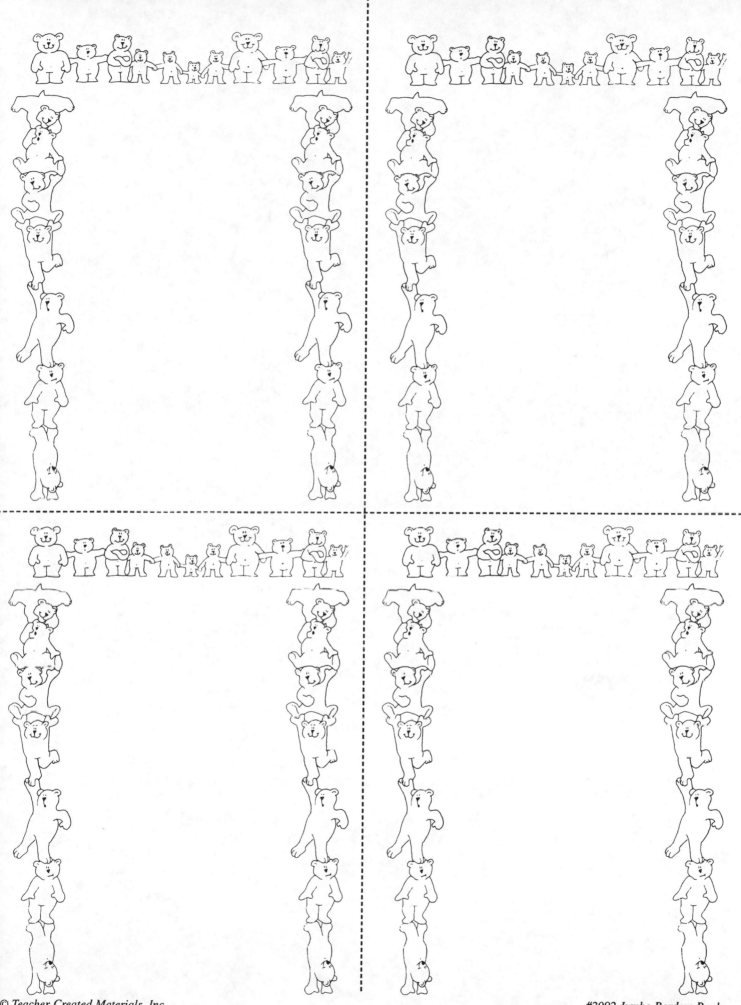

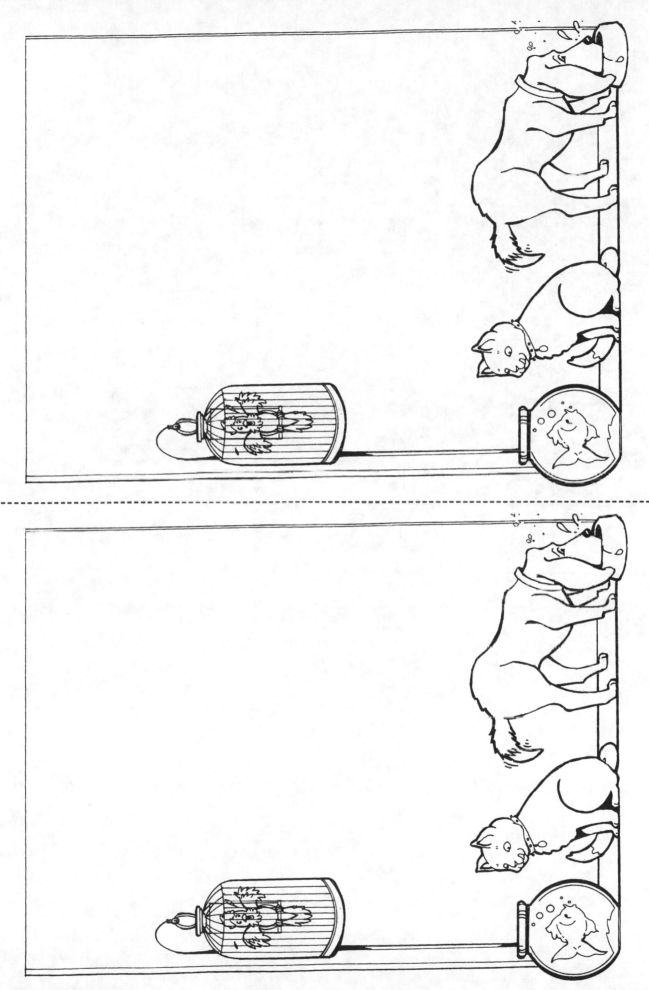

© Teacher Created Materials, Inc.

#2092 Jumbo Borders Book

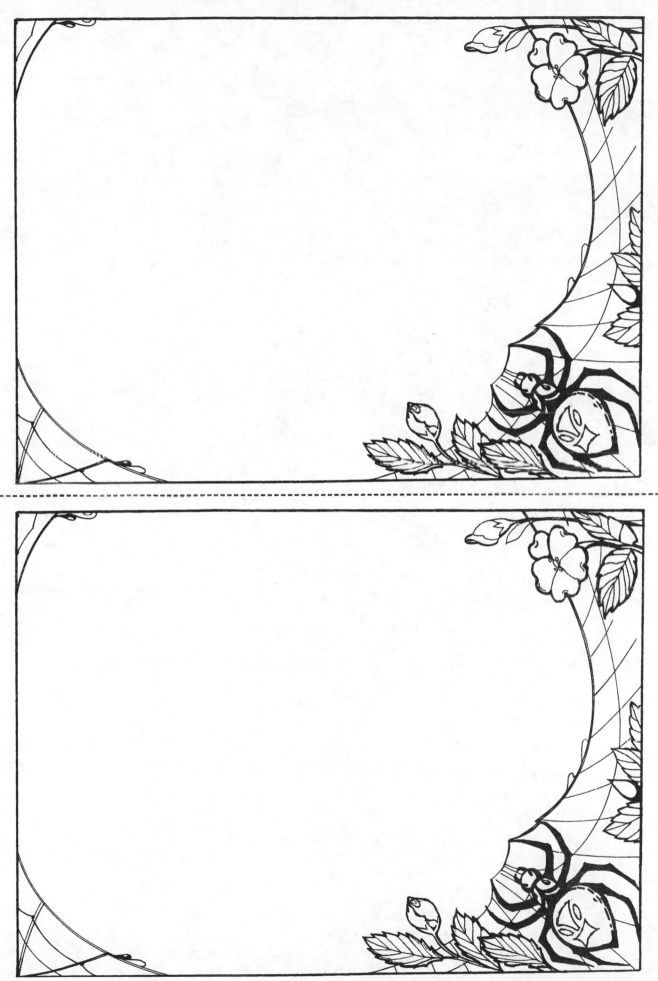

© Teacher Created Materials, Inc.

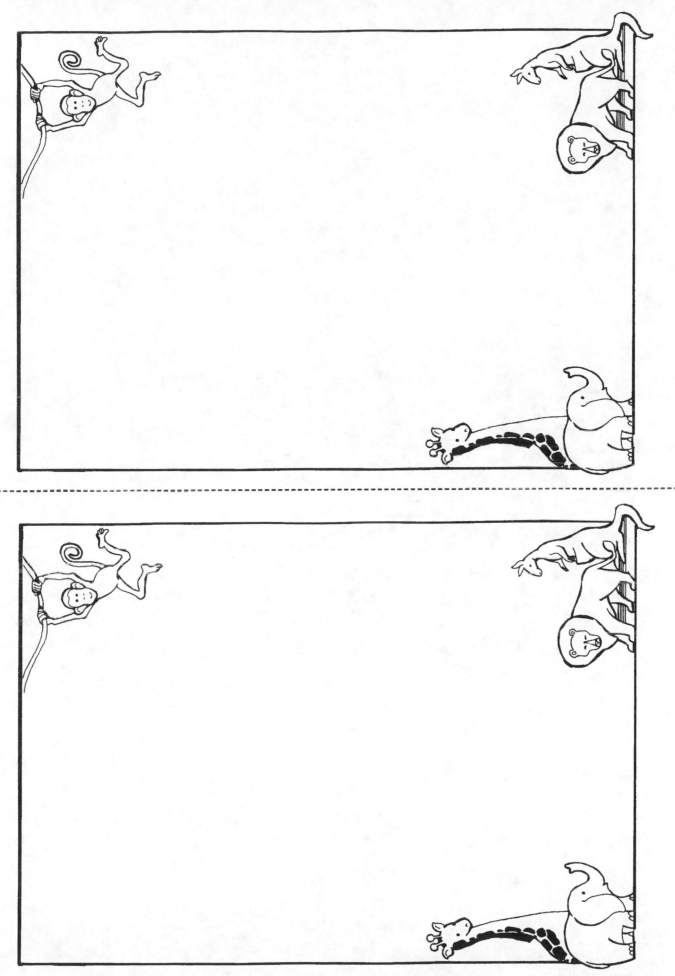

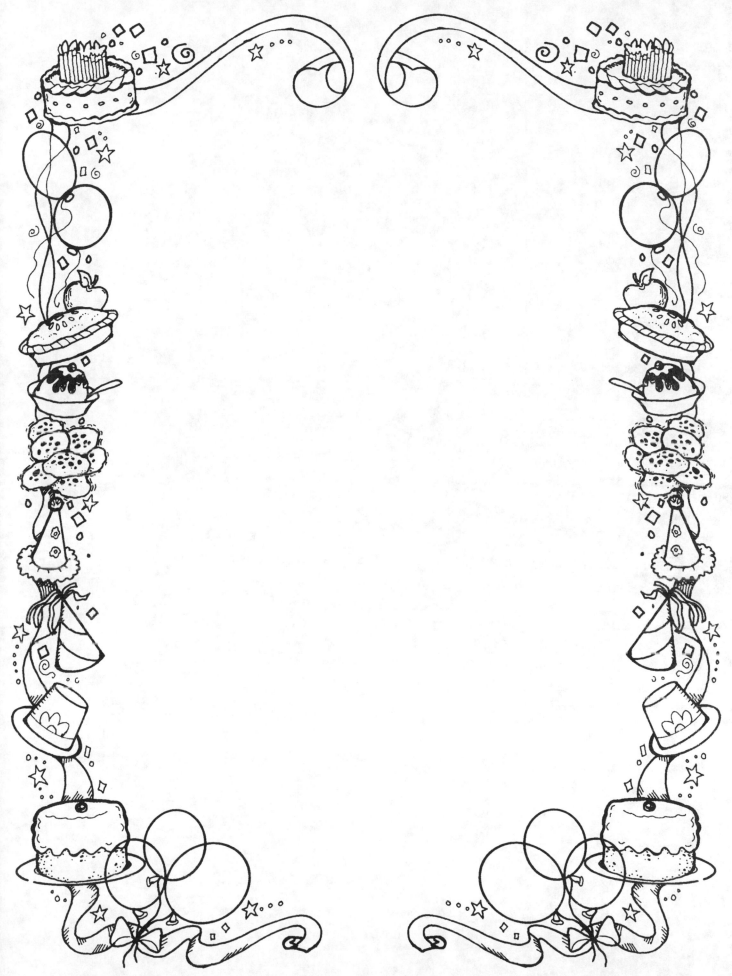

#2092 Jumbo Borders Book

Happy Birthday

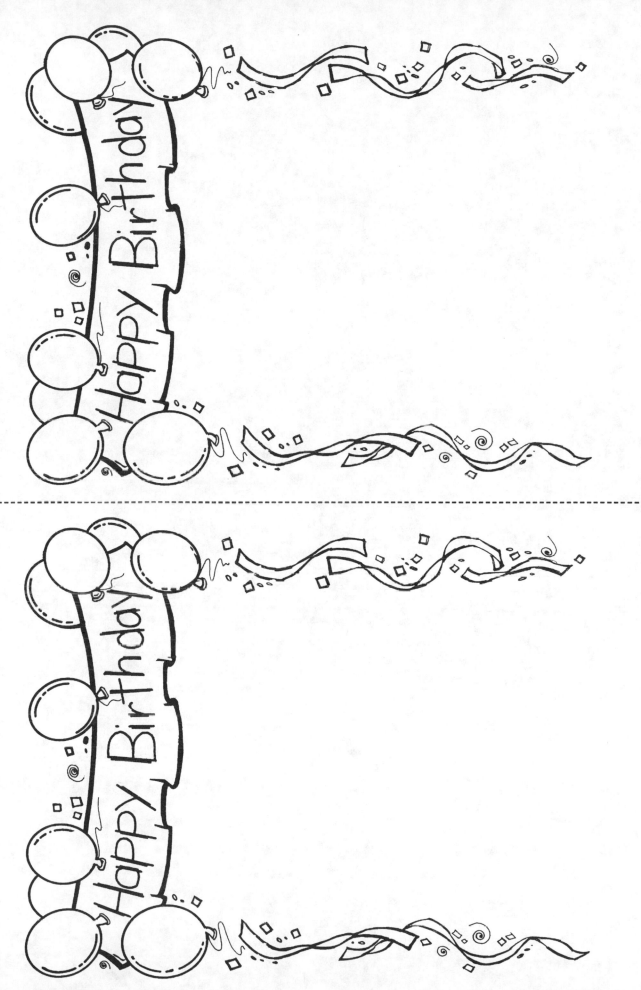

#2092 Jumbo Borders Book

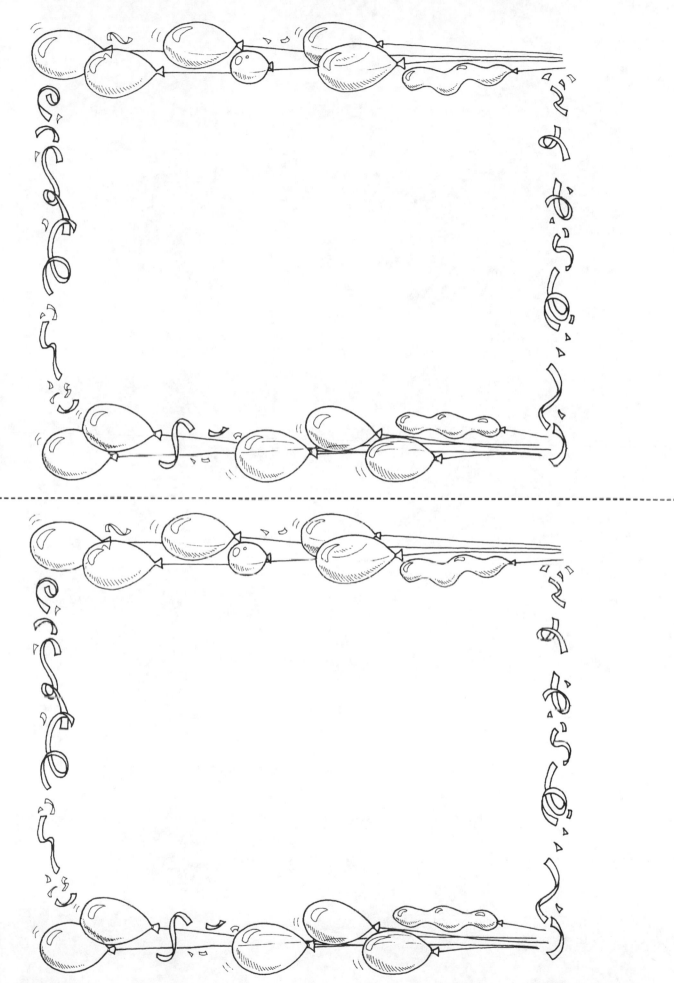

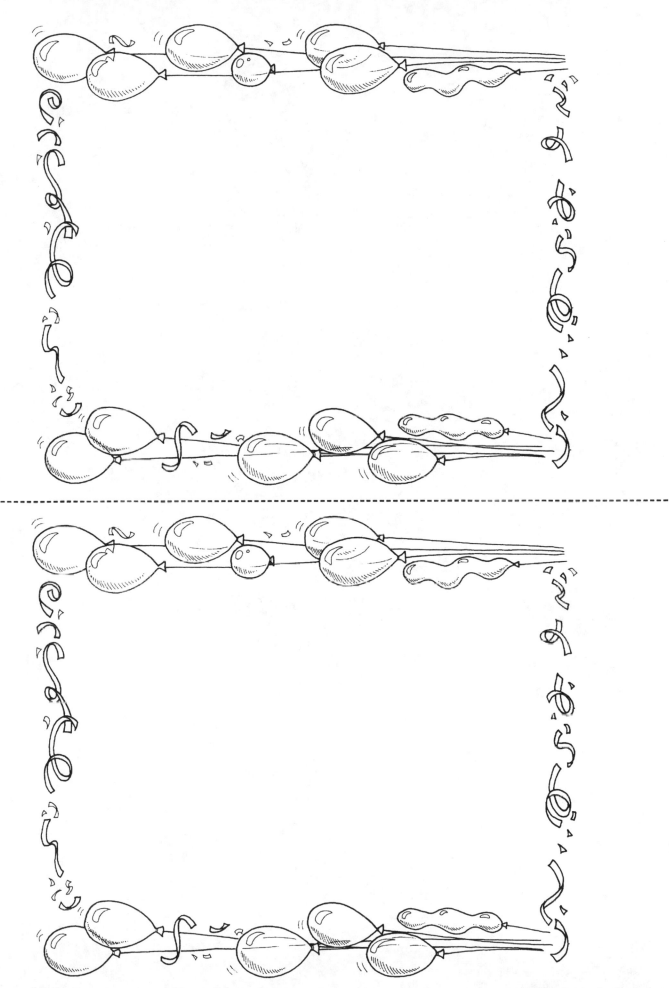

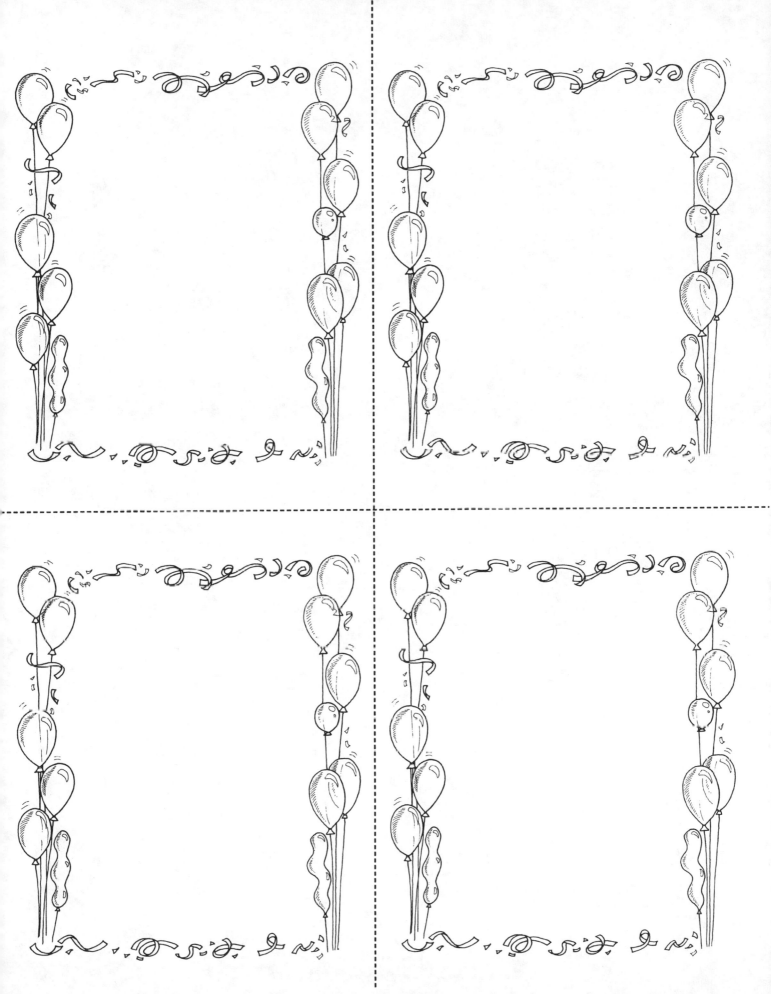

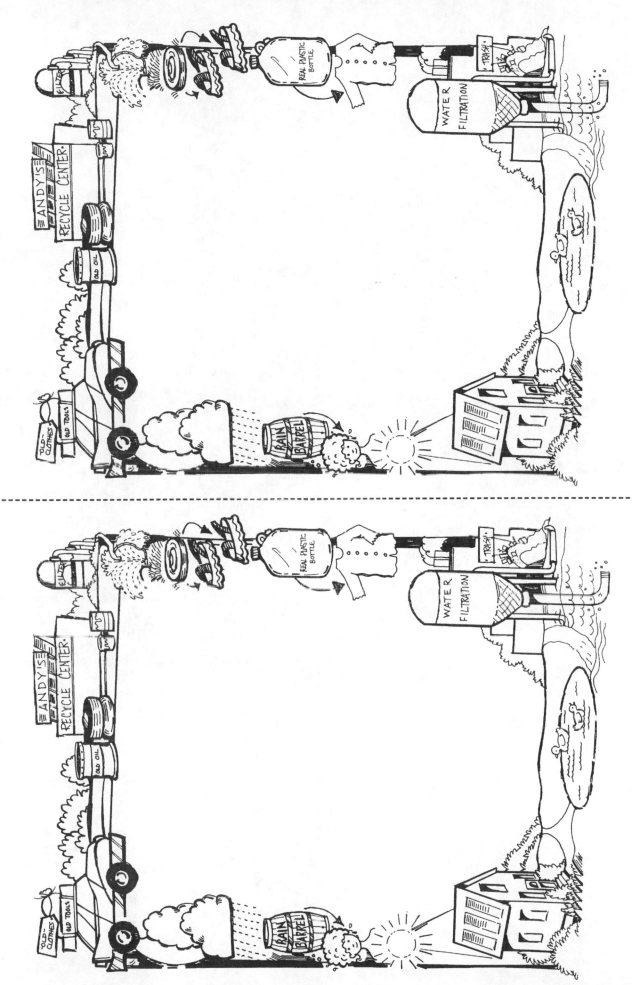

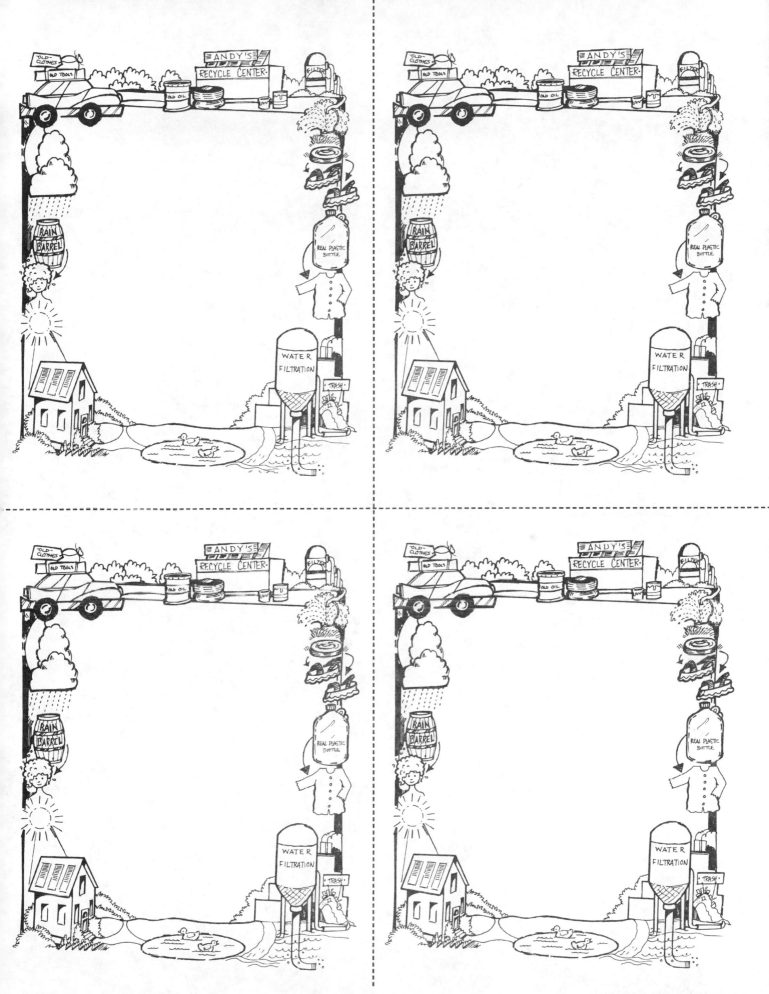

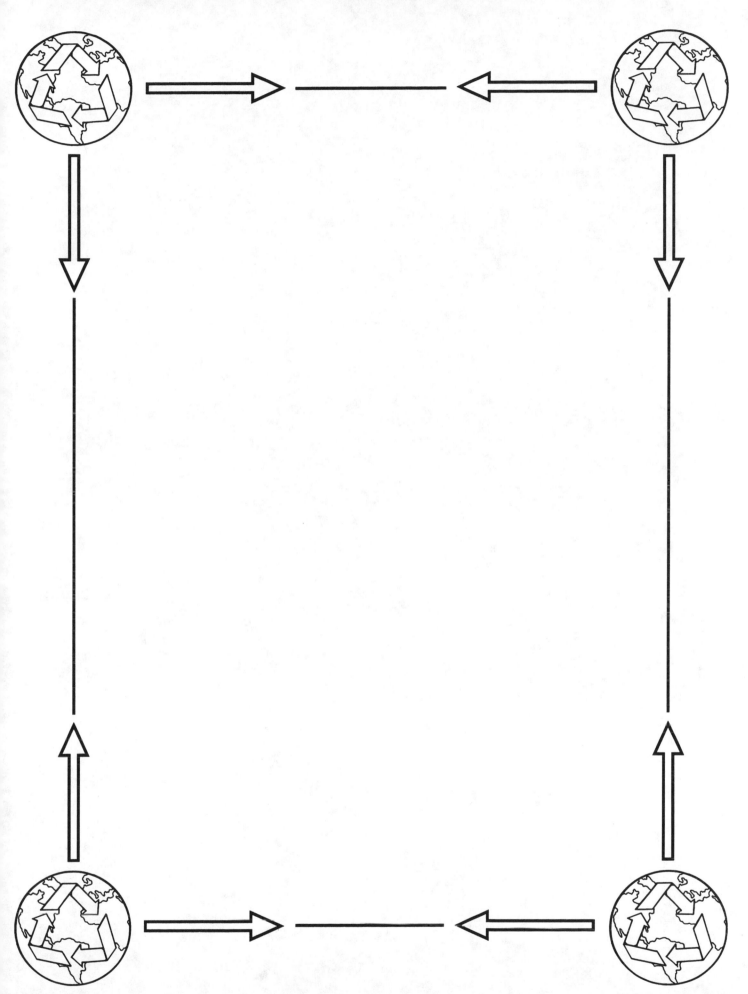

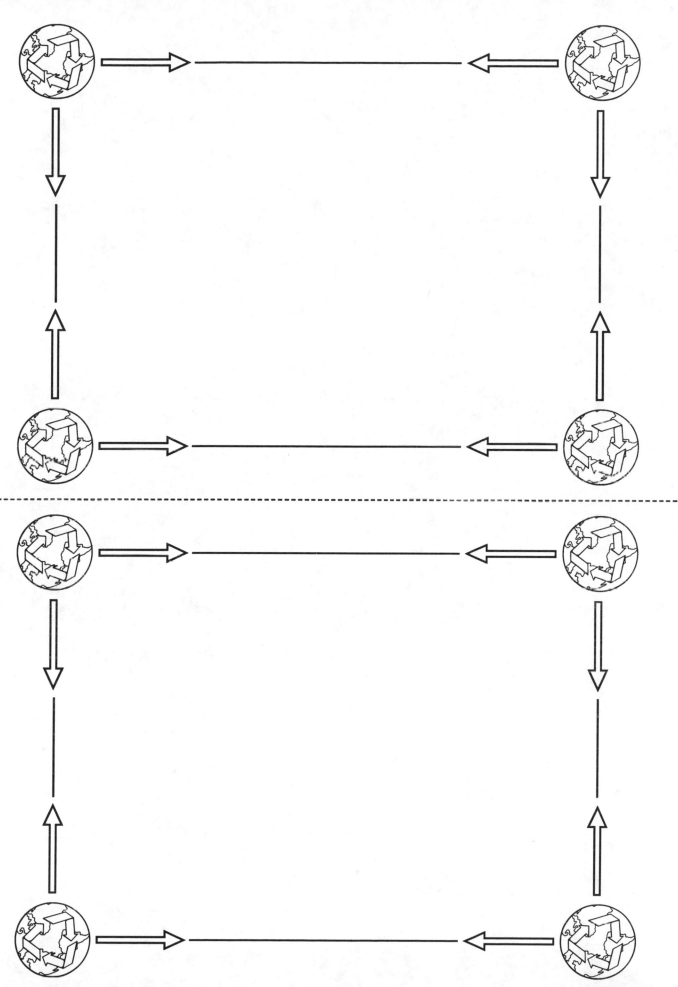

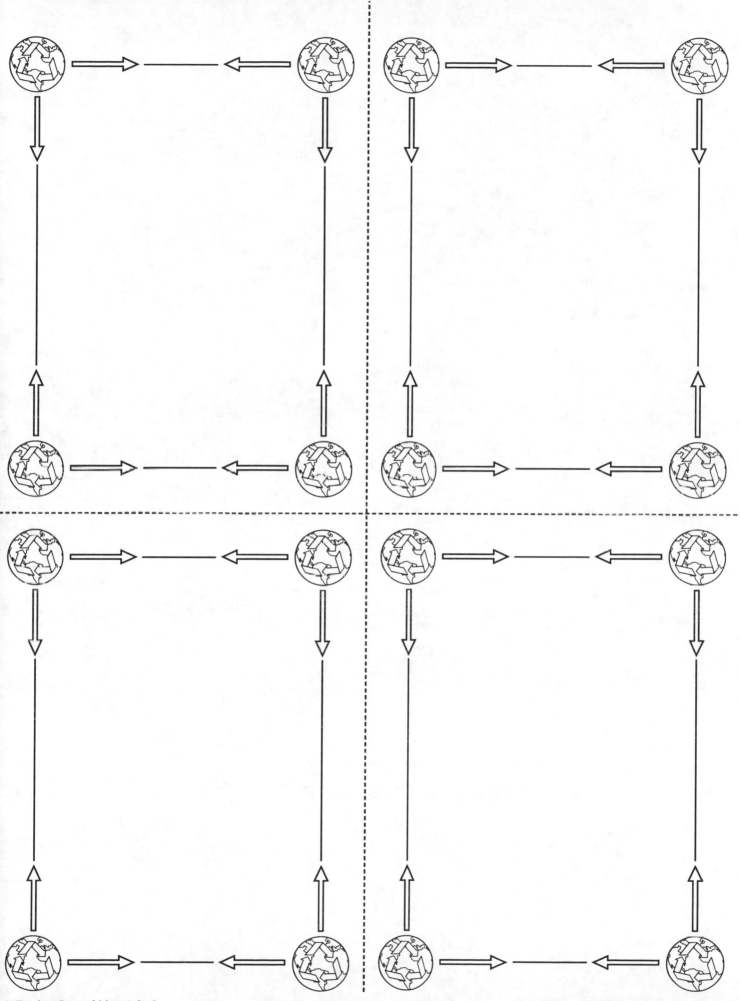

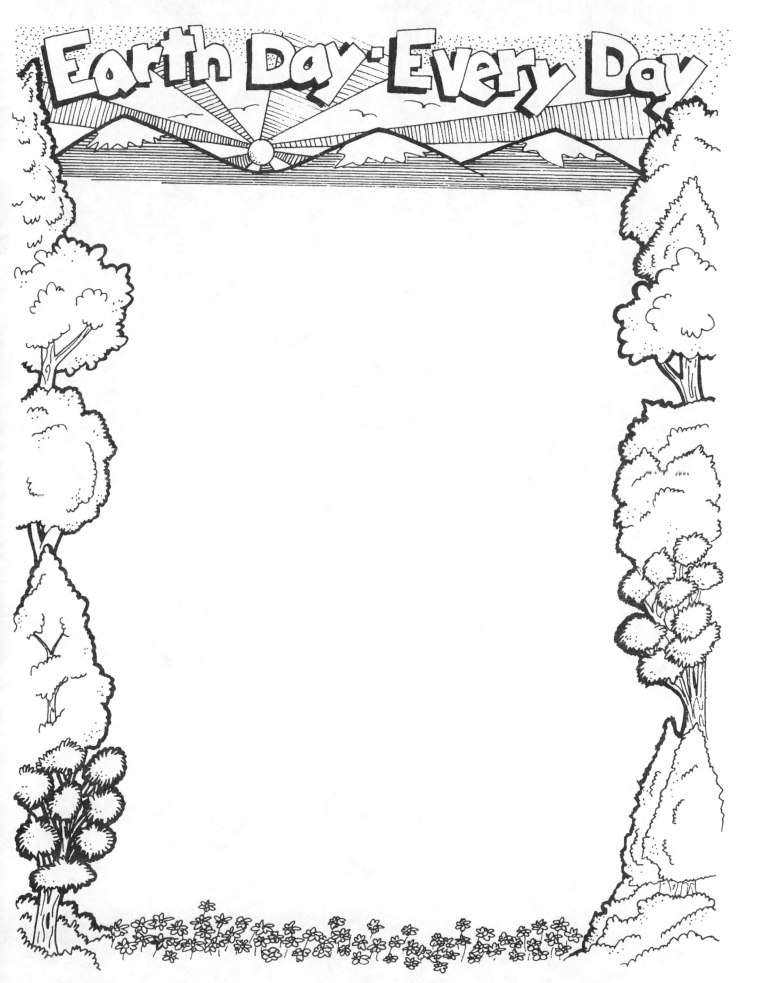

Earth Day · Every Day

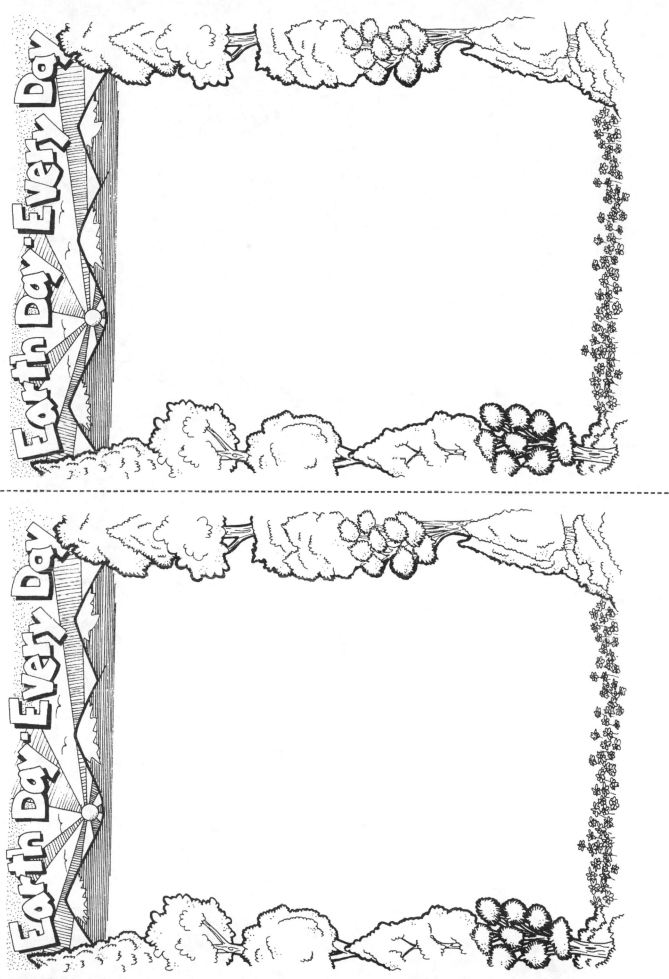

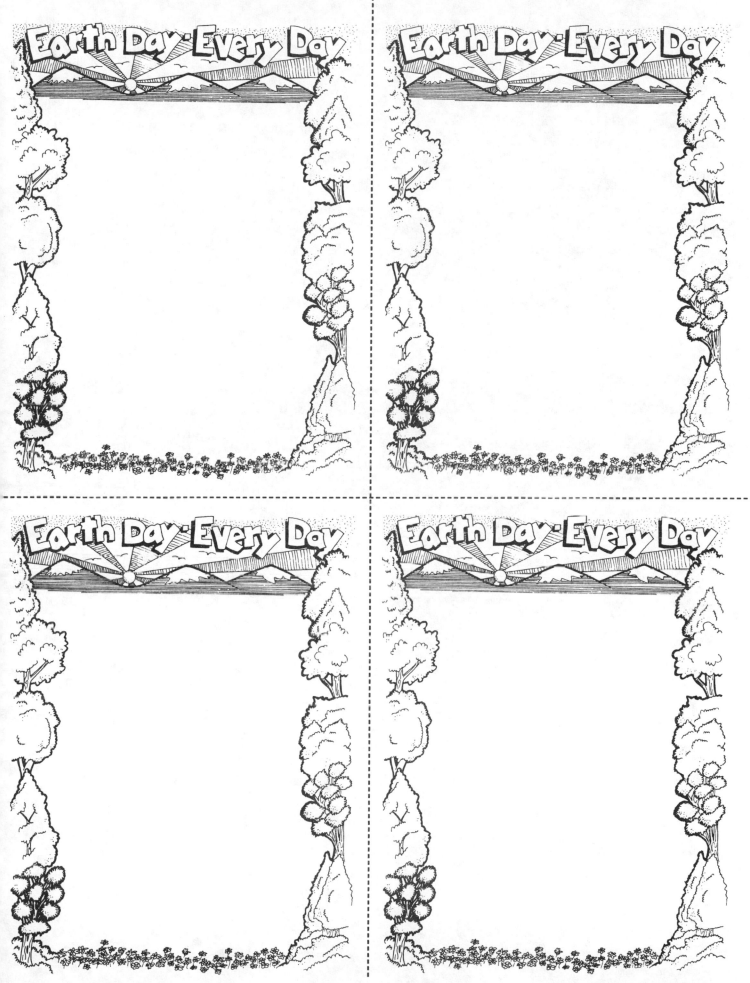

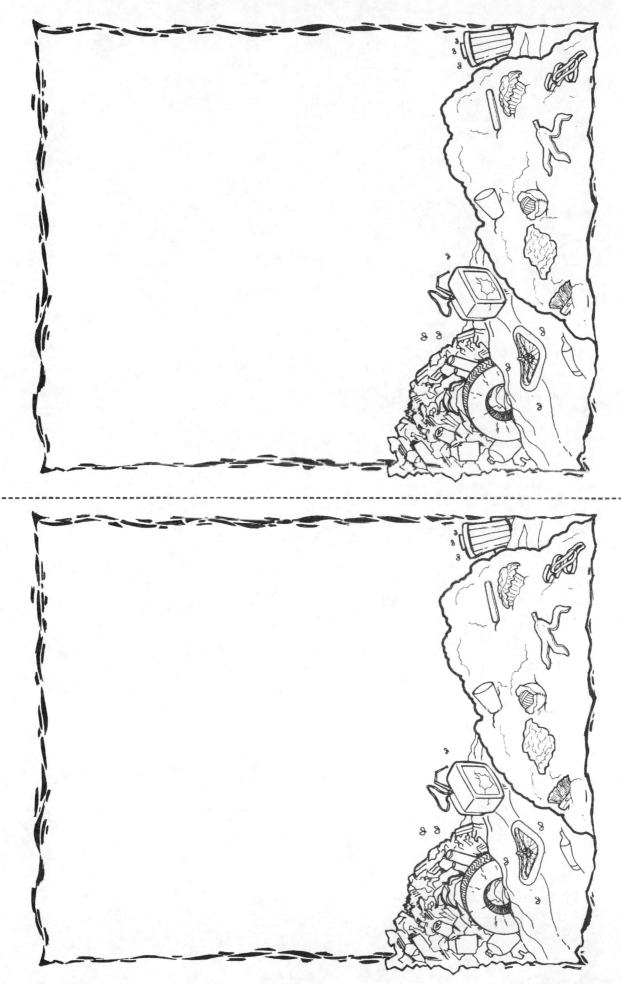

#2092 Jumbo Borders Book

CANDY · STORE

Jellybeans

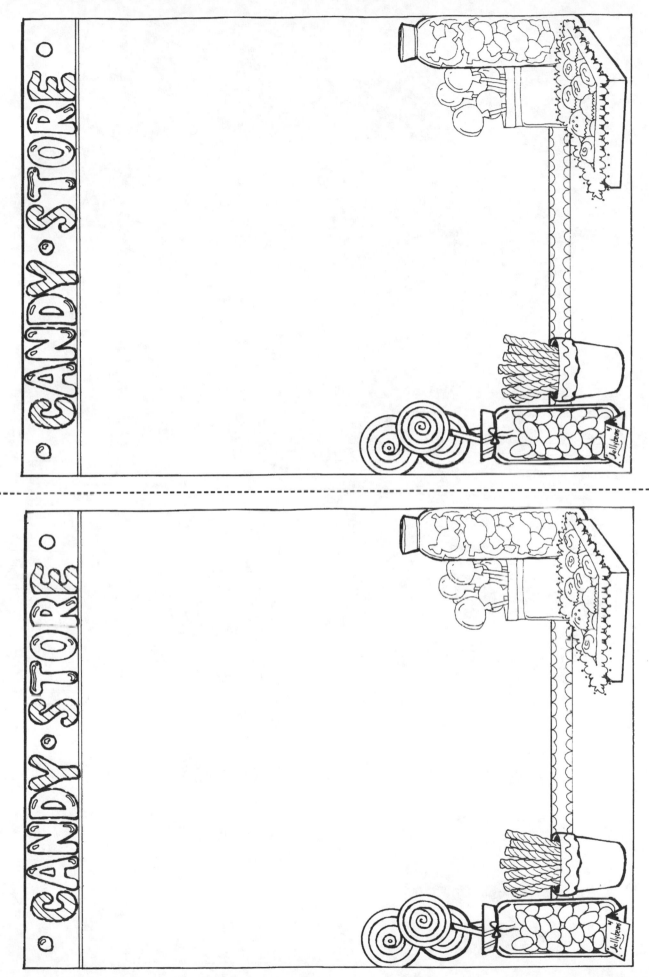

#2092 Jumbo Borders Book

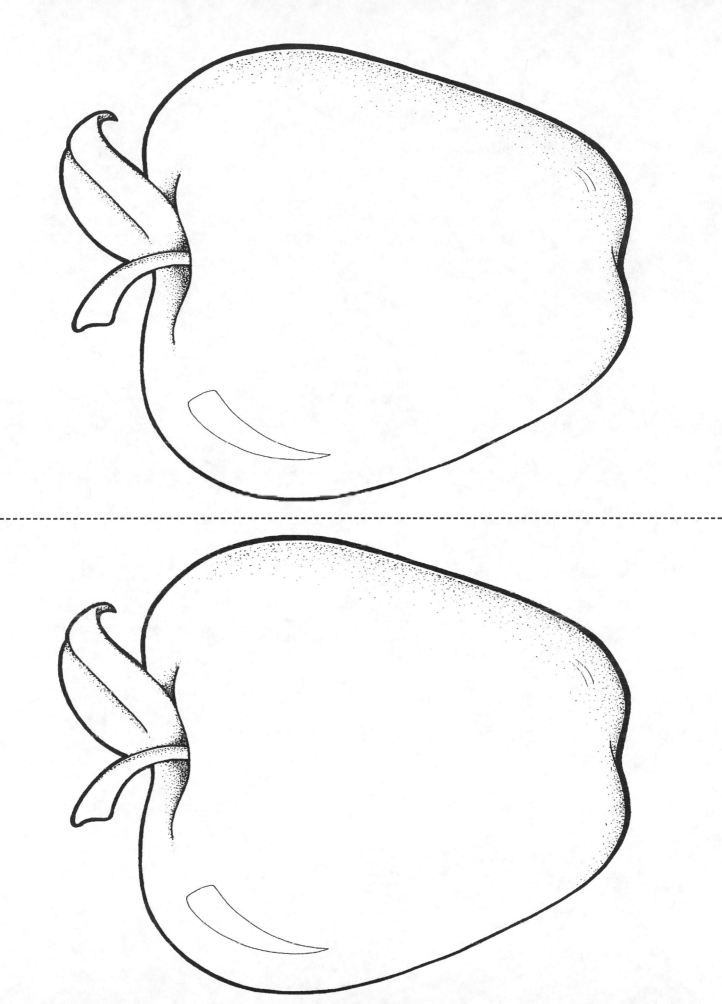

© Teacher Created Materials, Inc.

#2092 Jumbo Borders Book

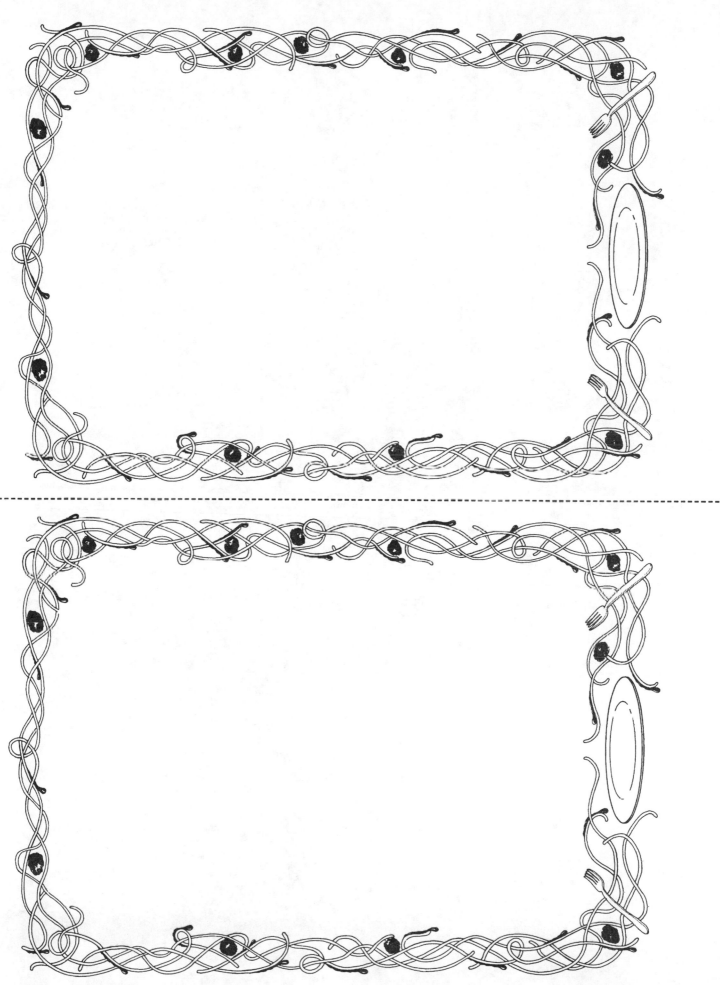

© Teacher Created Materials, Inc.

#2092 Jumbo Borders Book

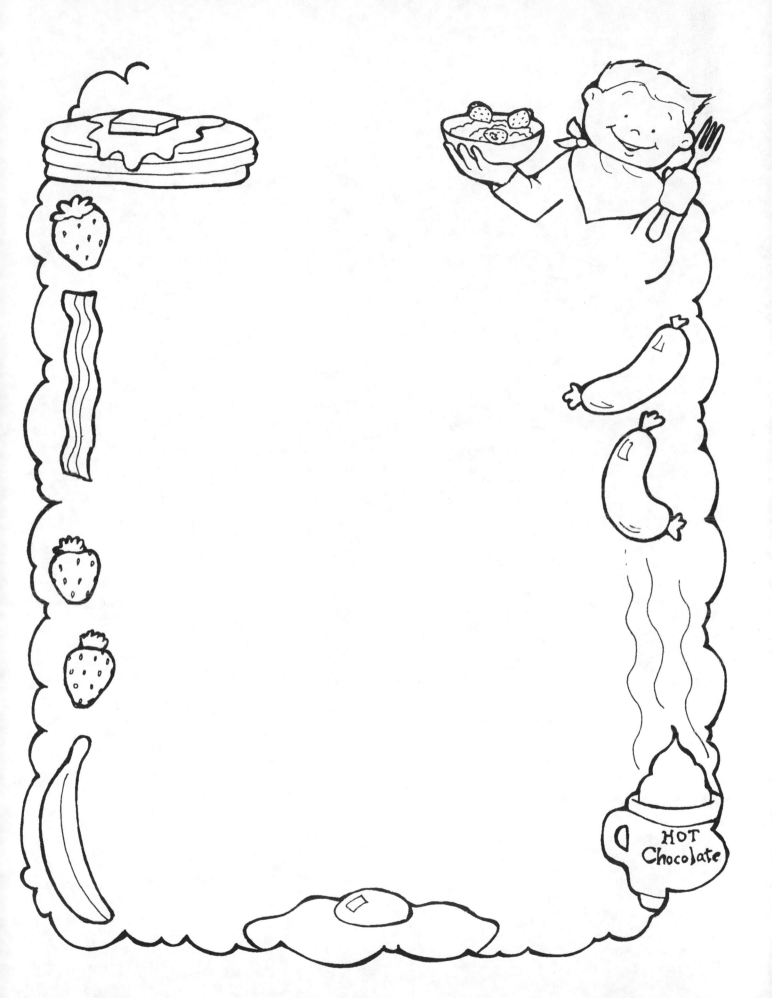

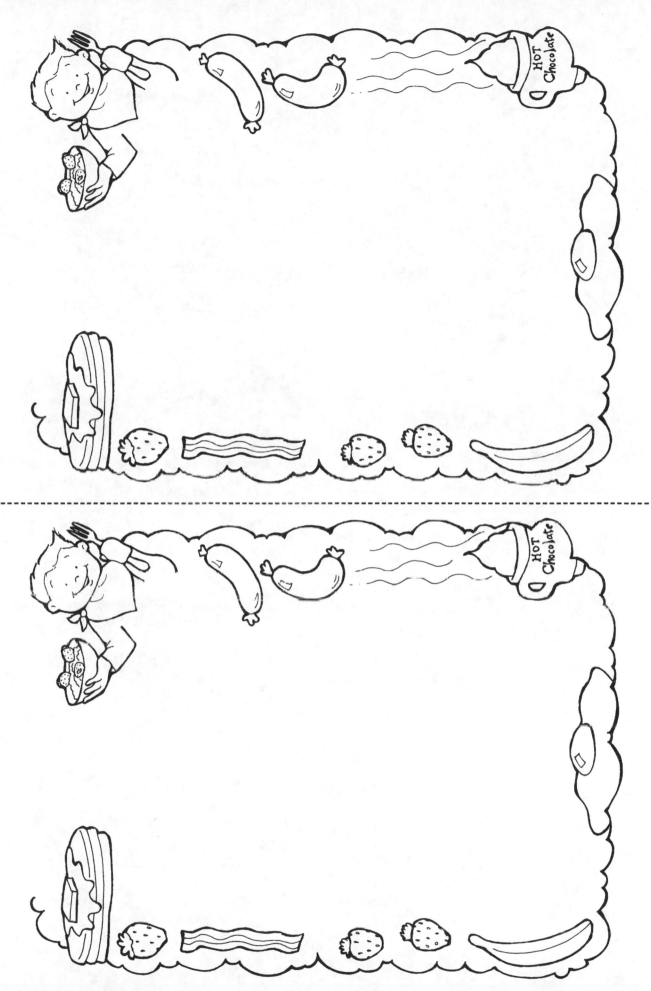

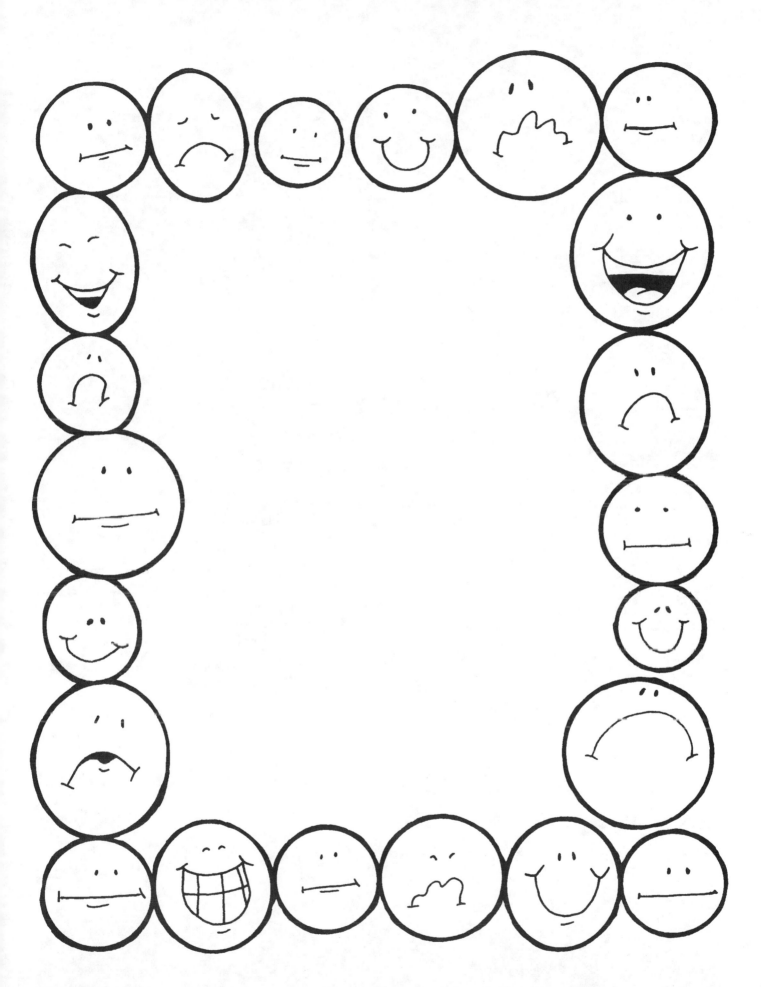

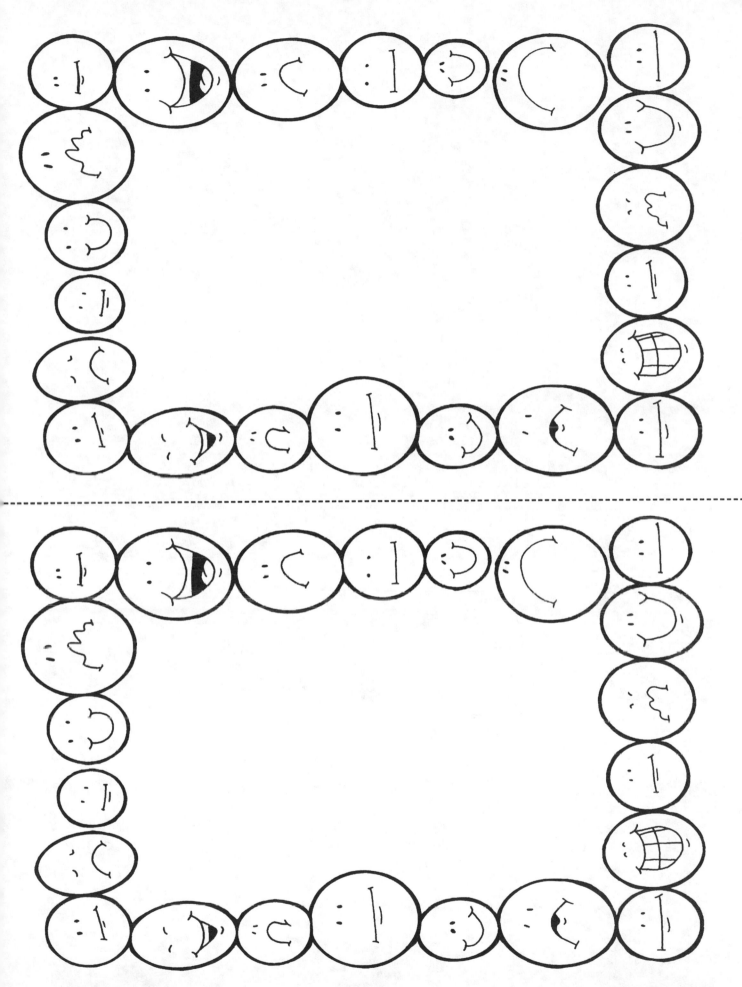

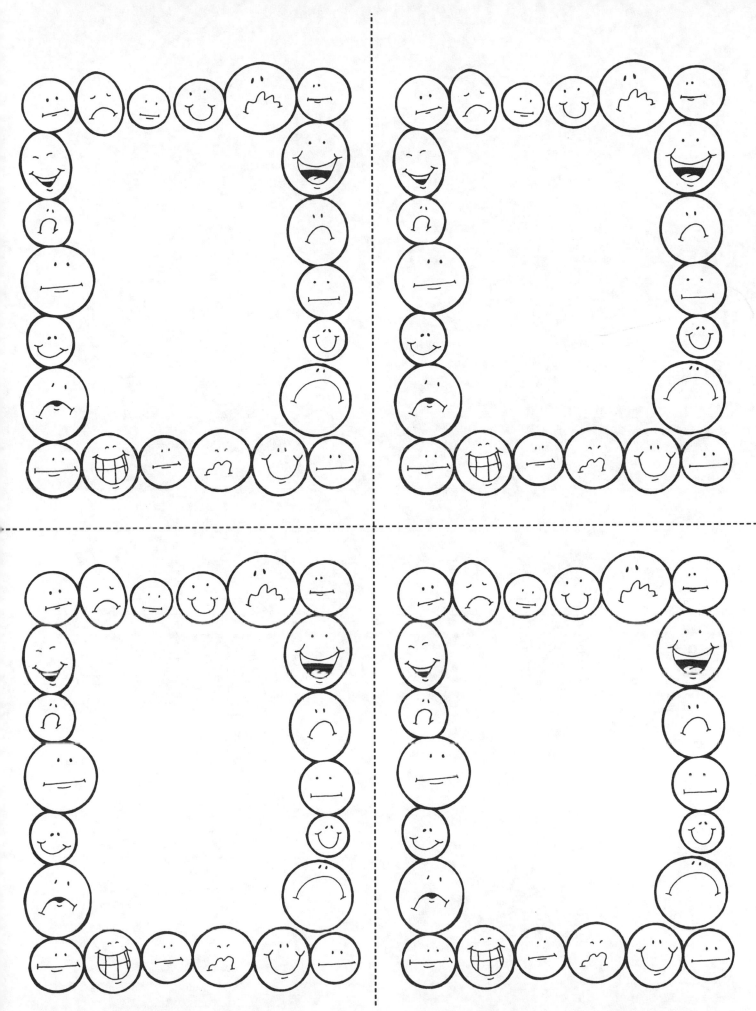

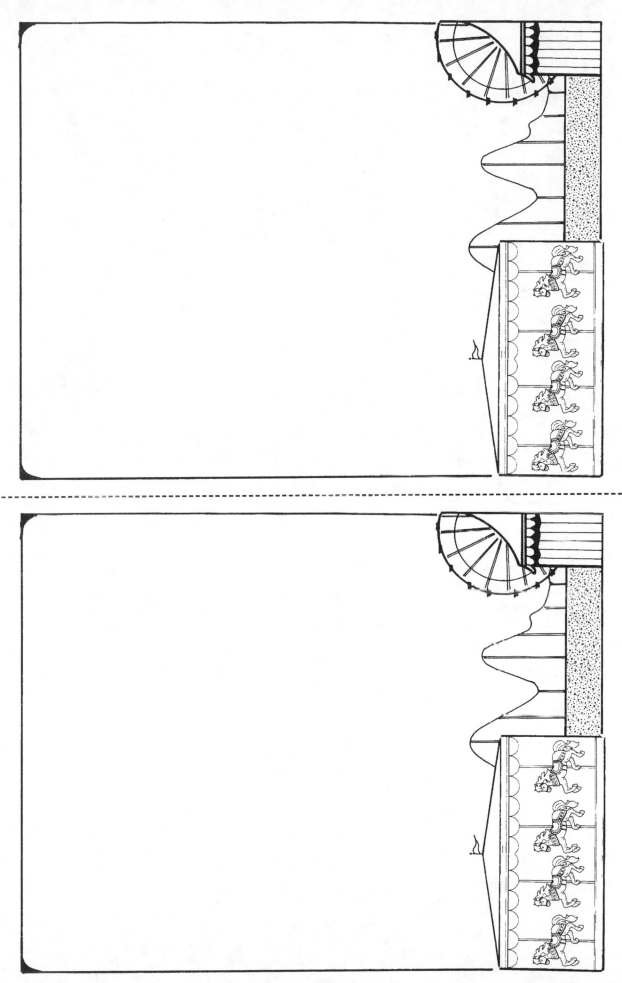

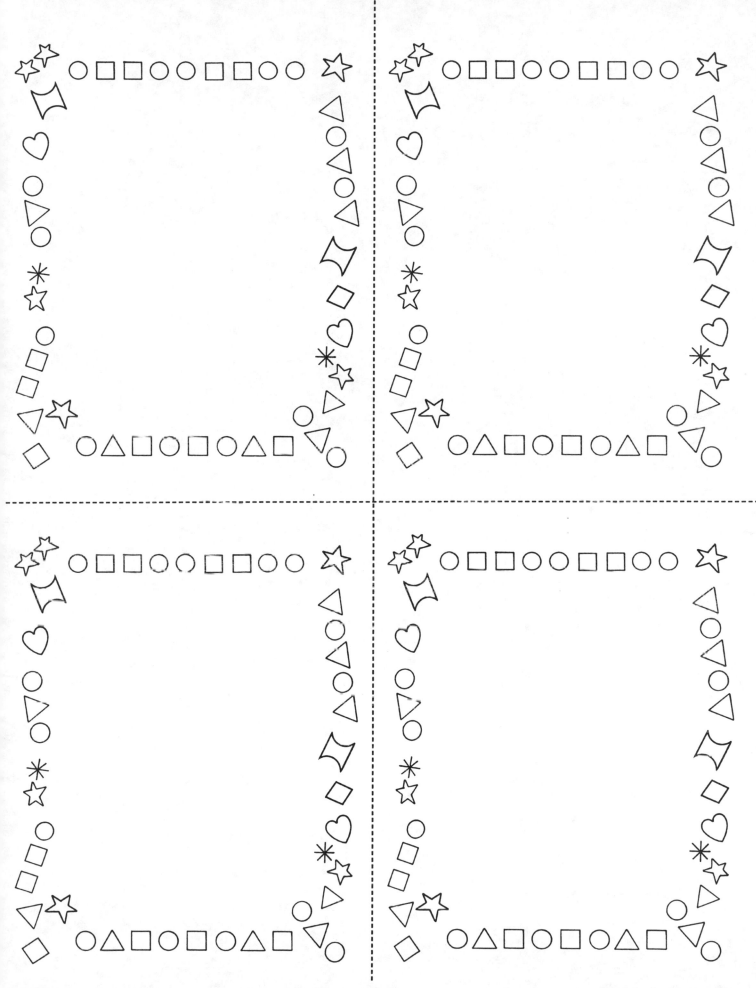

#2092 Jumbo Borders Book

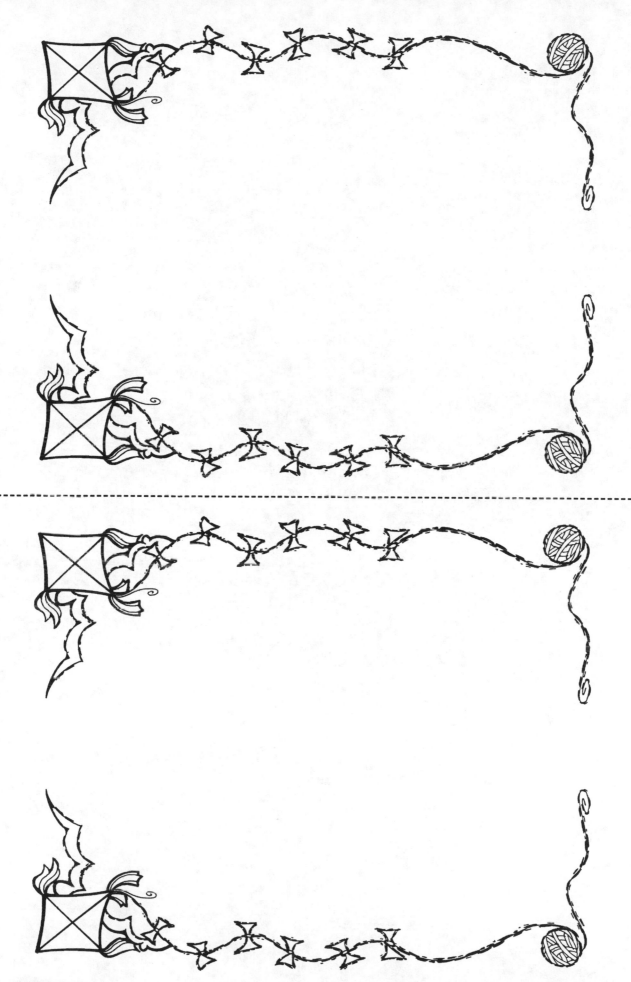

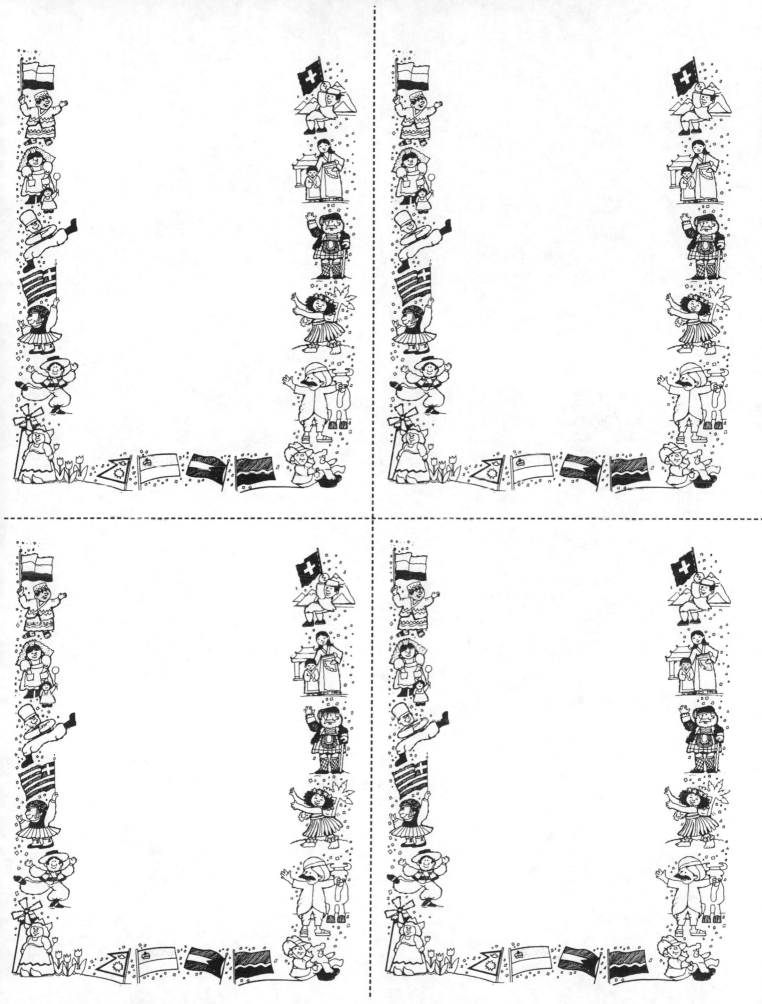

#2092 Jumbo Borders Book

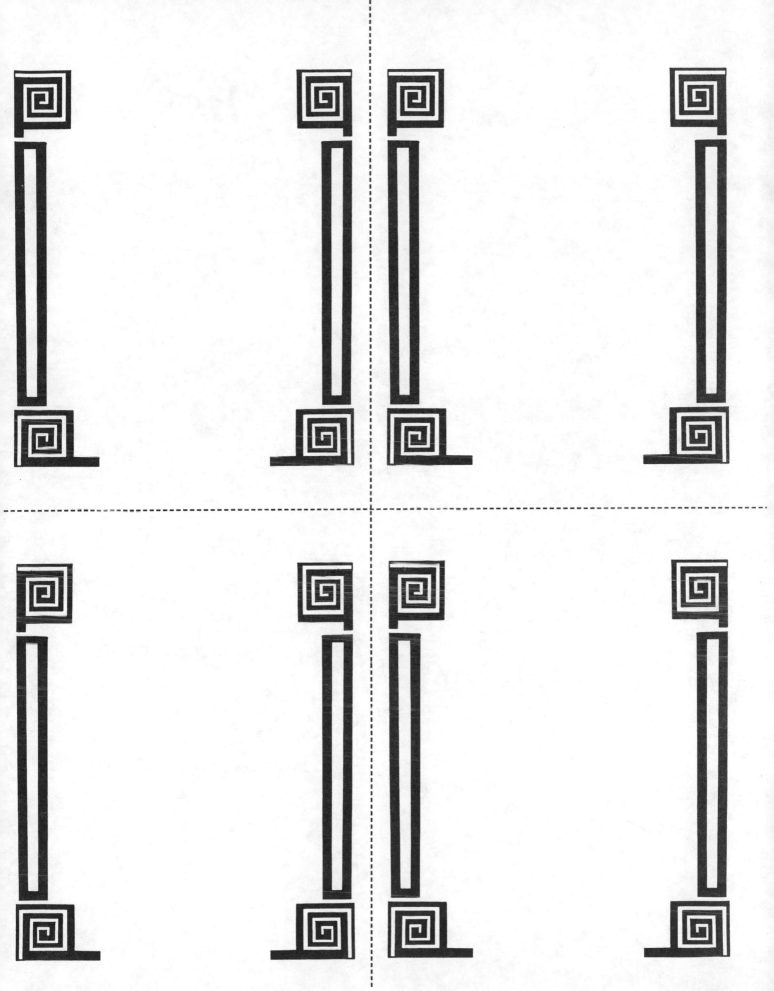

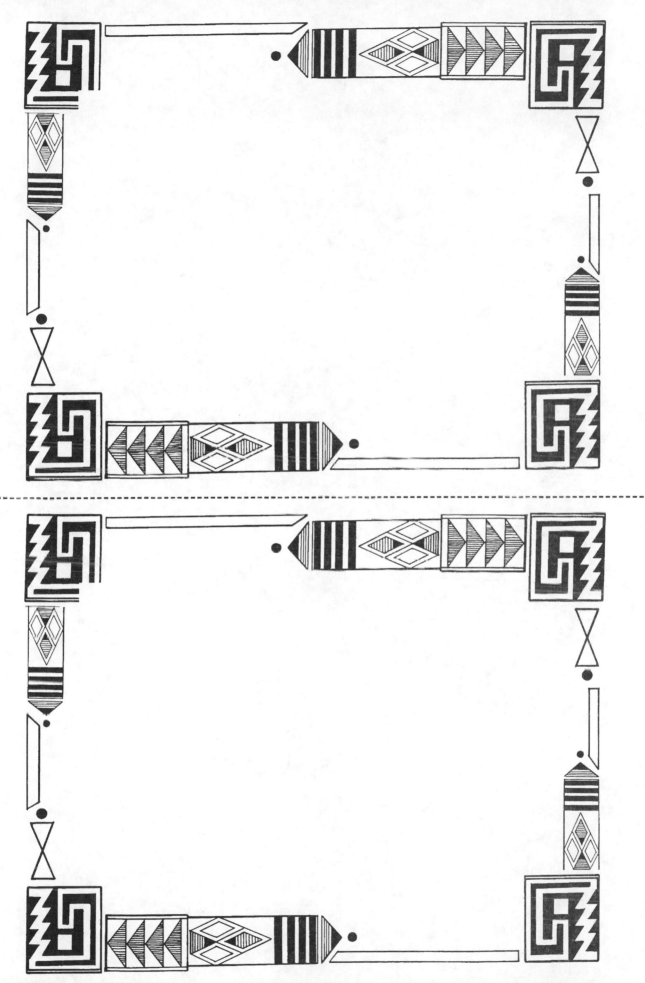

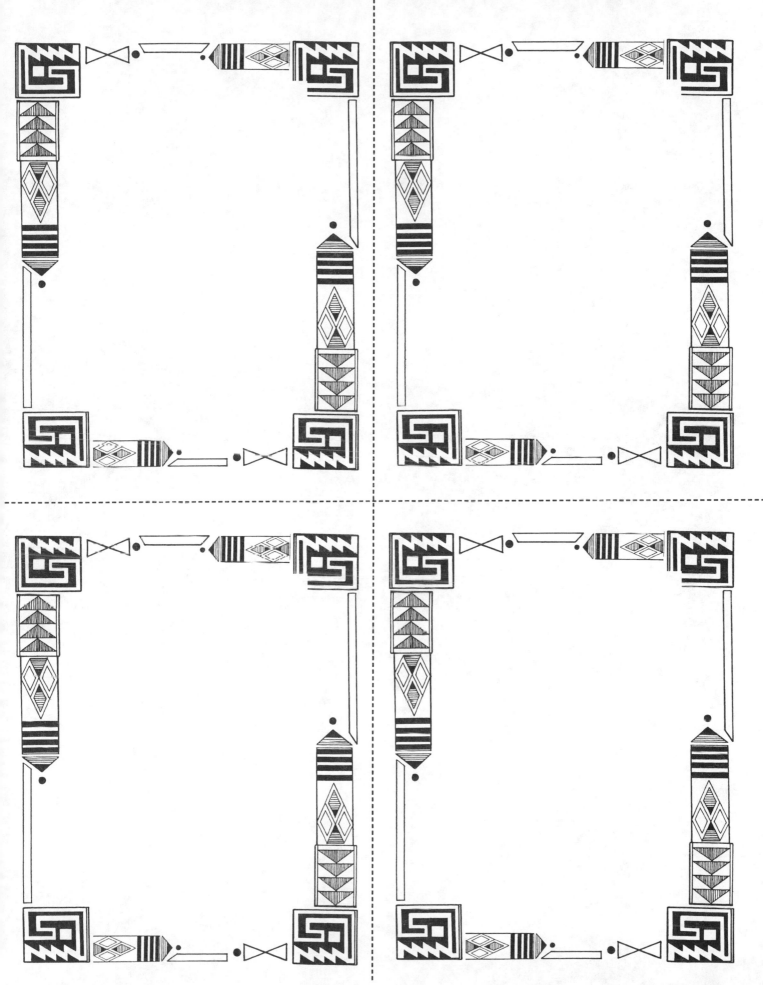

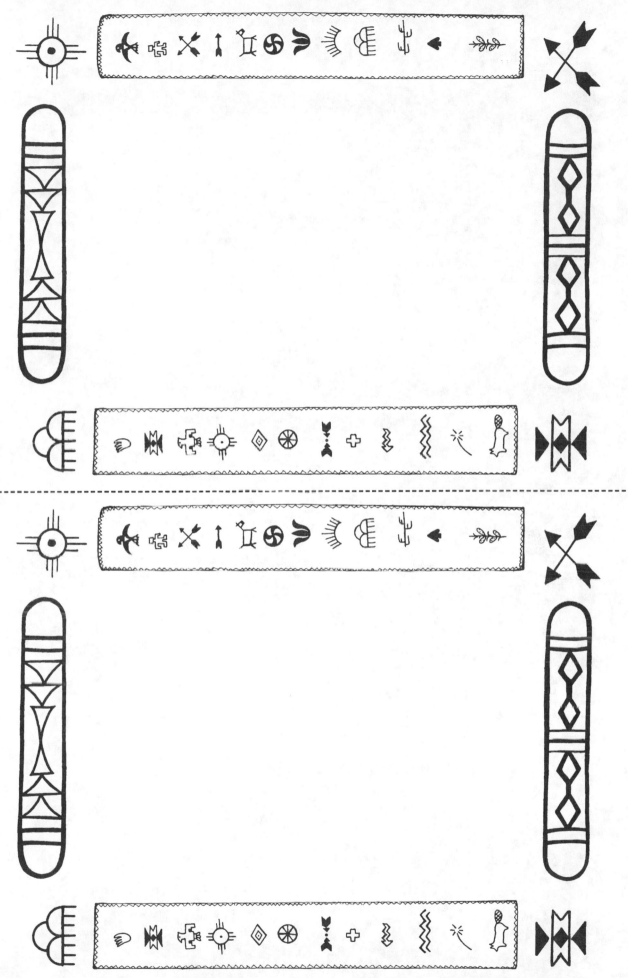

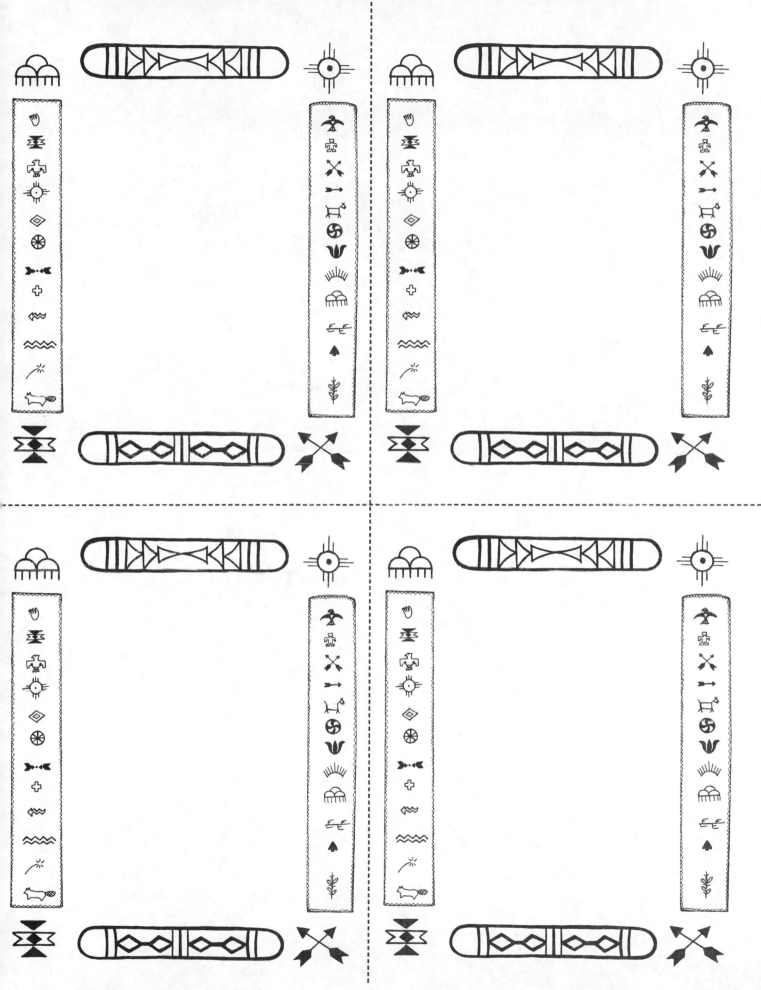

#2092 Jumbo Borders Book

#2092 Jumbo Borders Book

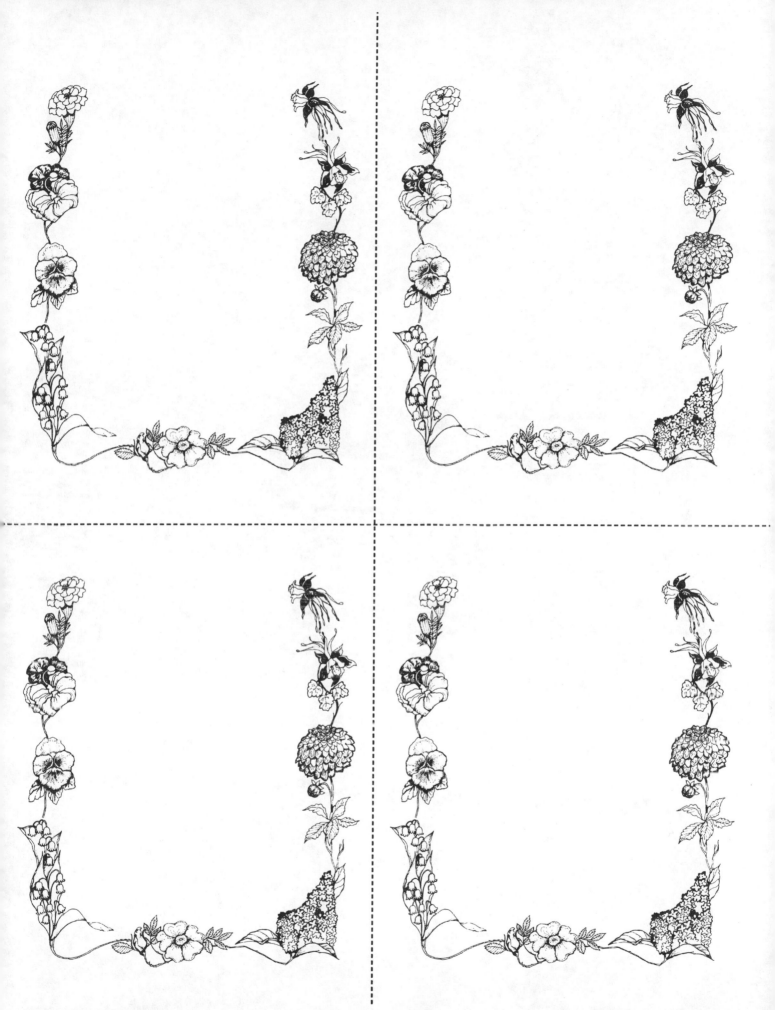

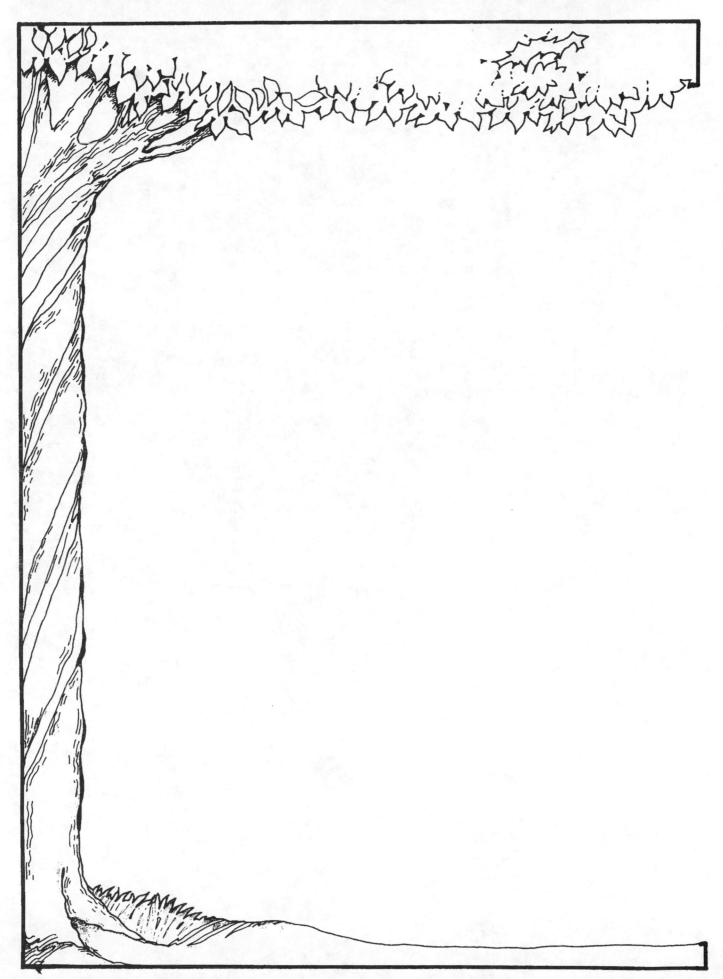

© Teacher Created Materials, Inc.

#2092 Jumbo Borders Book

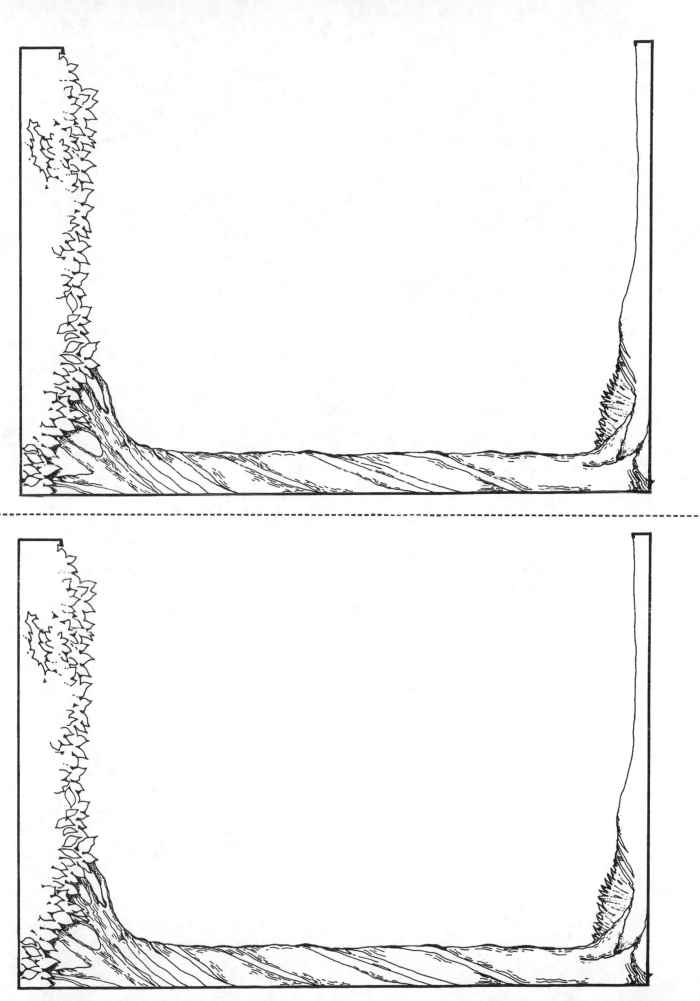

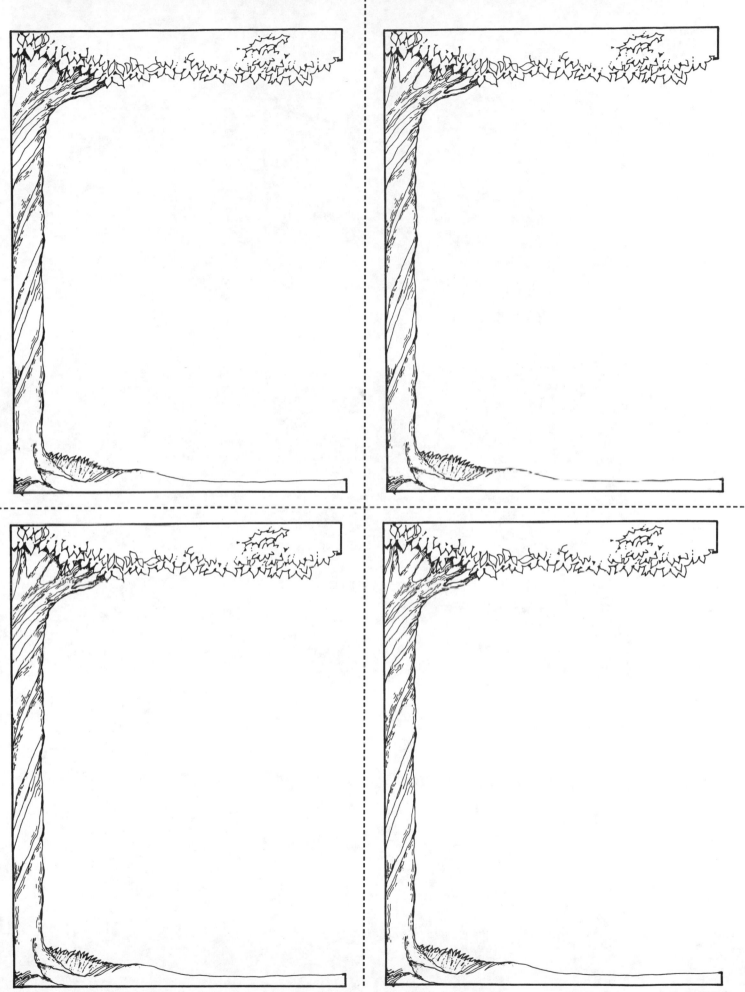

#2092 Jumbo Borders Book

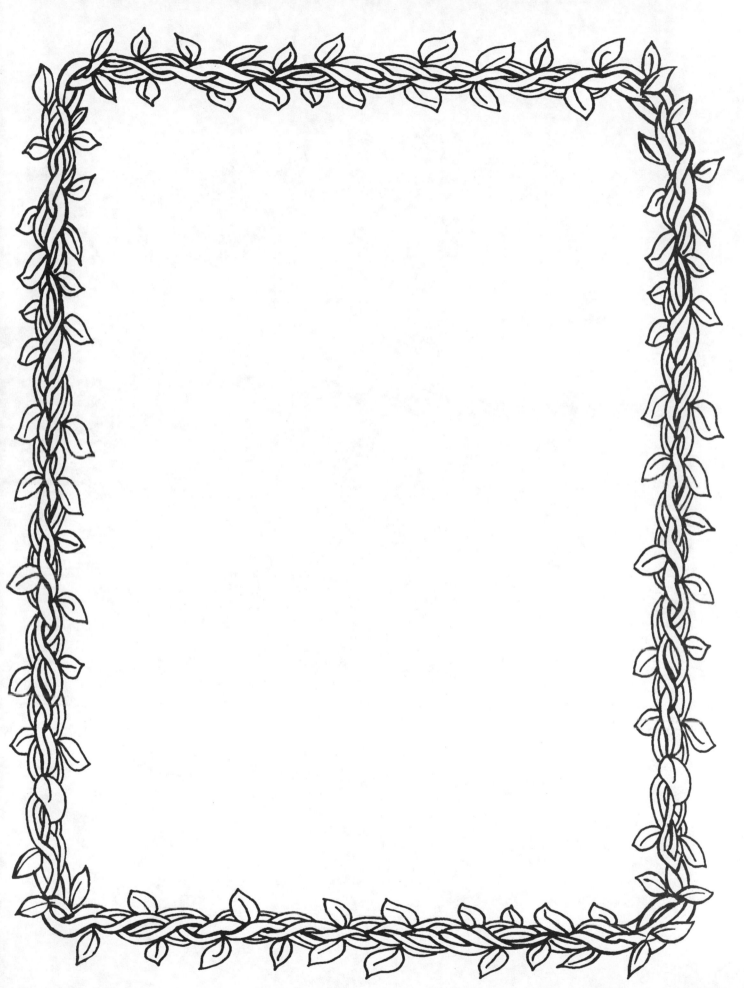

© Teacher Created Materials, Inc.

#2092 Jumbo Borders Book

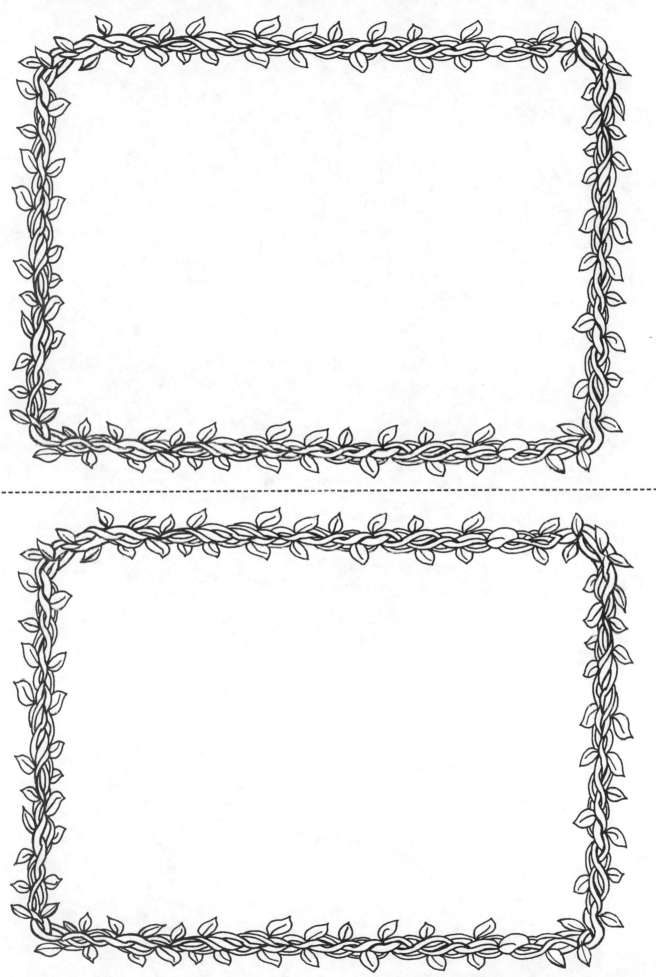

© Teacher Created Materials, Inc.

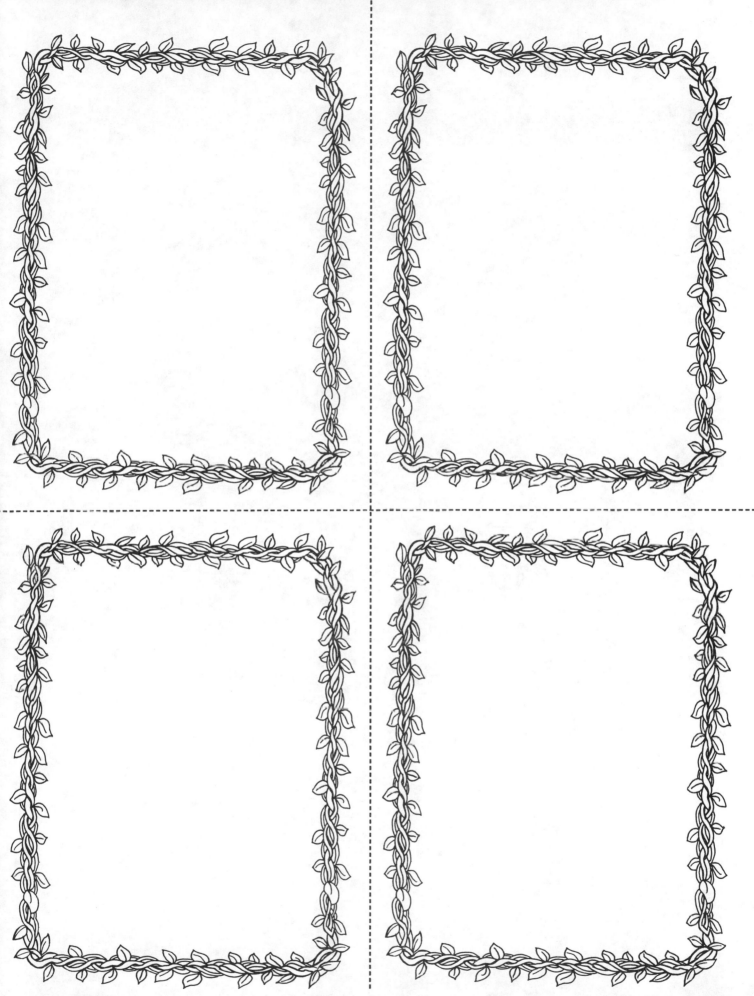

© *Teacher Created Materials, Inc.*

#2092 Jumbo Borders Book

© Teacher Created Materials, Inc.

#2092 Jumbo Borders Book

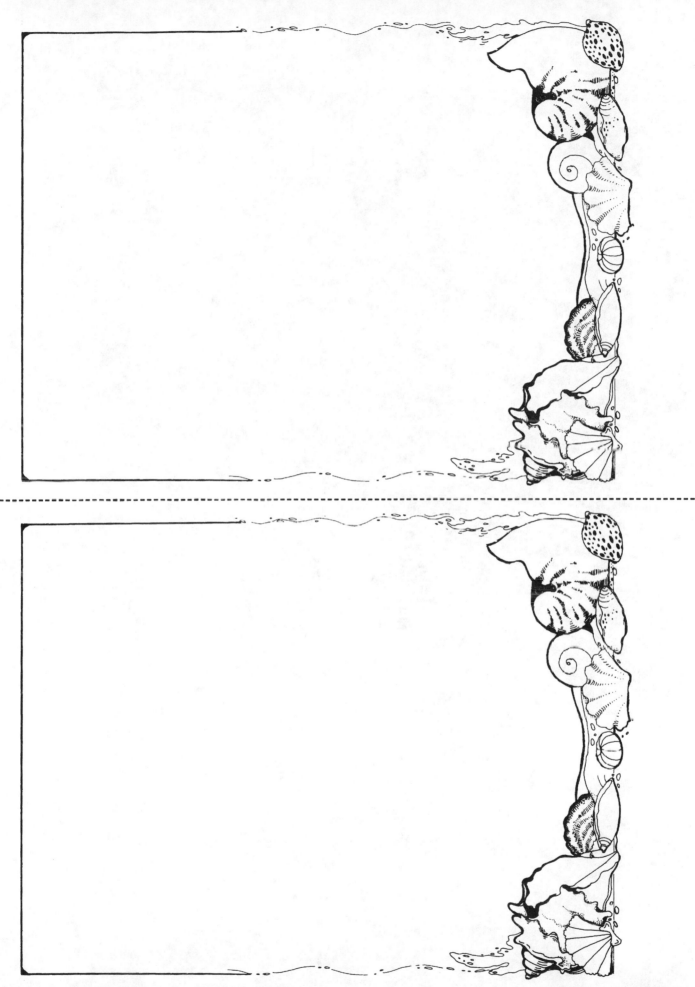

© Teacher Created Materials, Inc.

#2092 Jumbo Borders Book

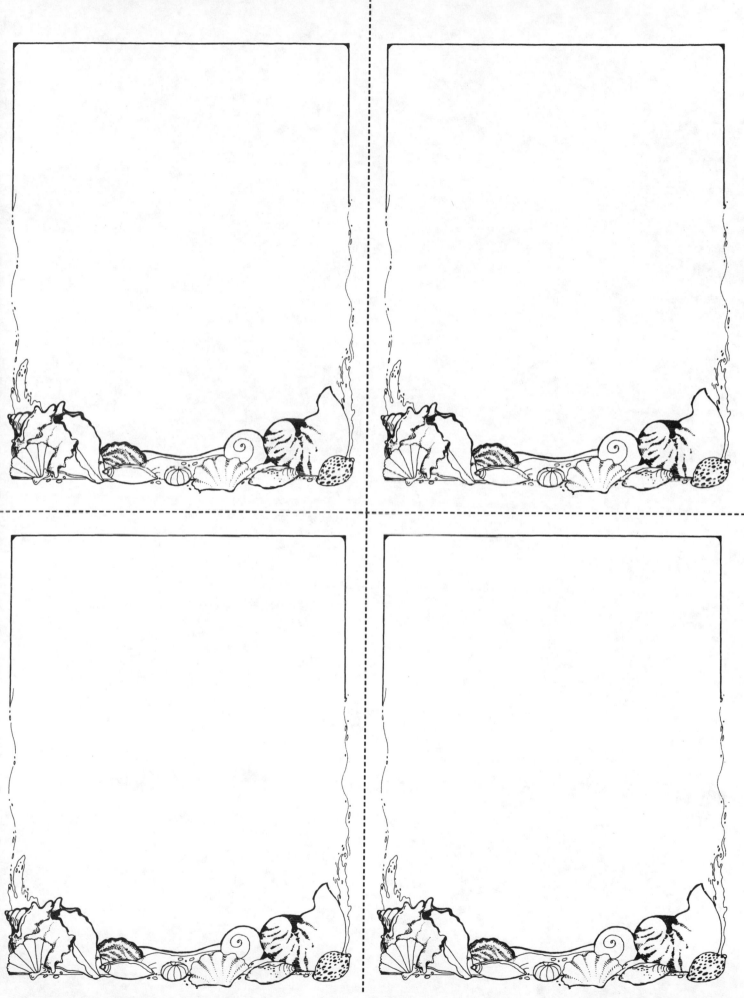

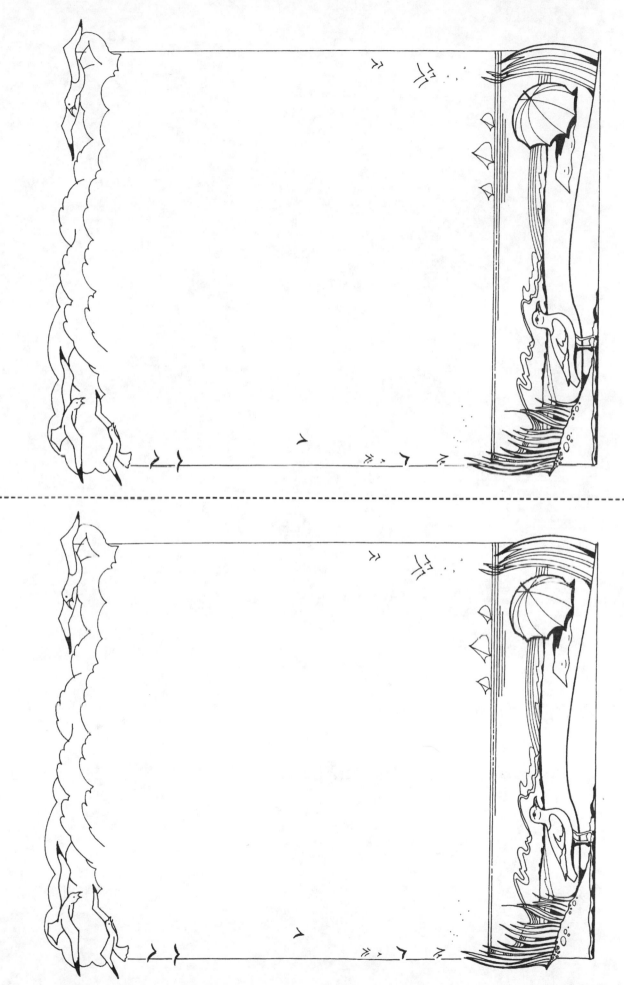

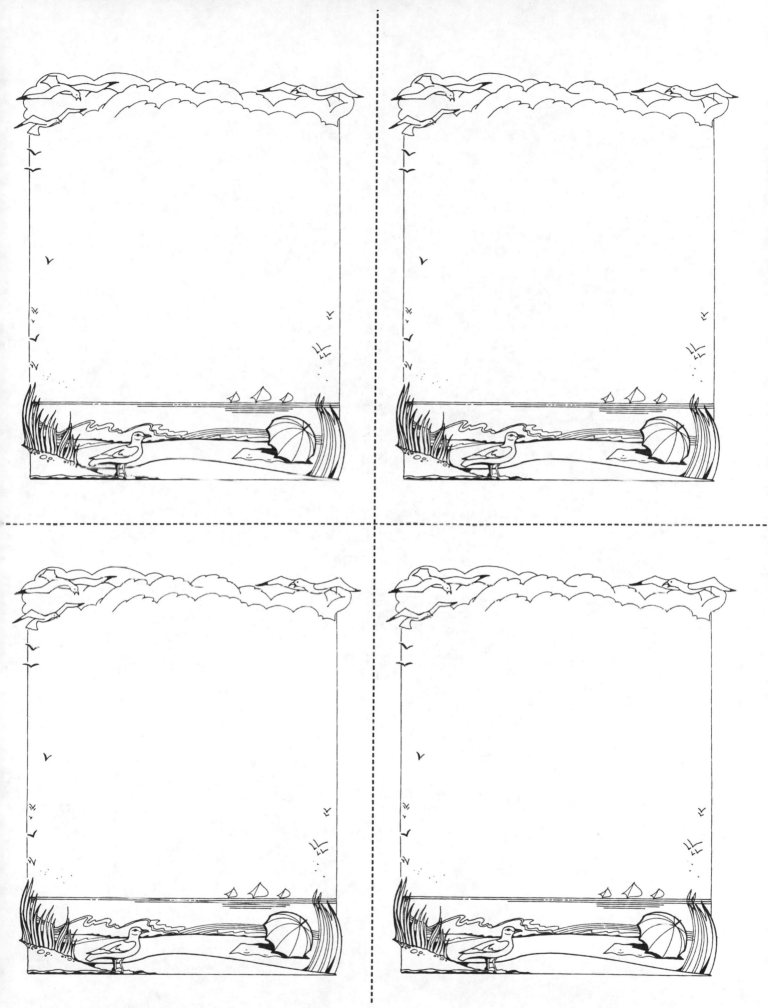

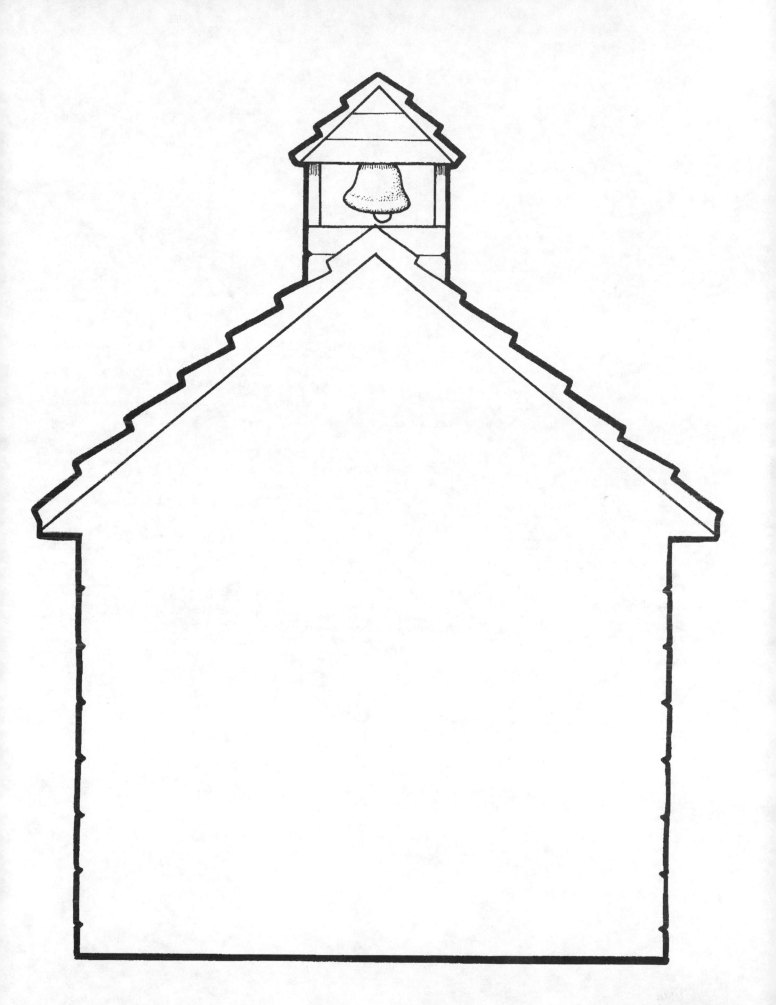

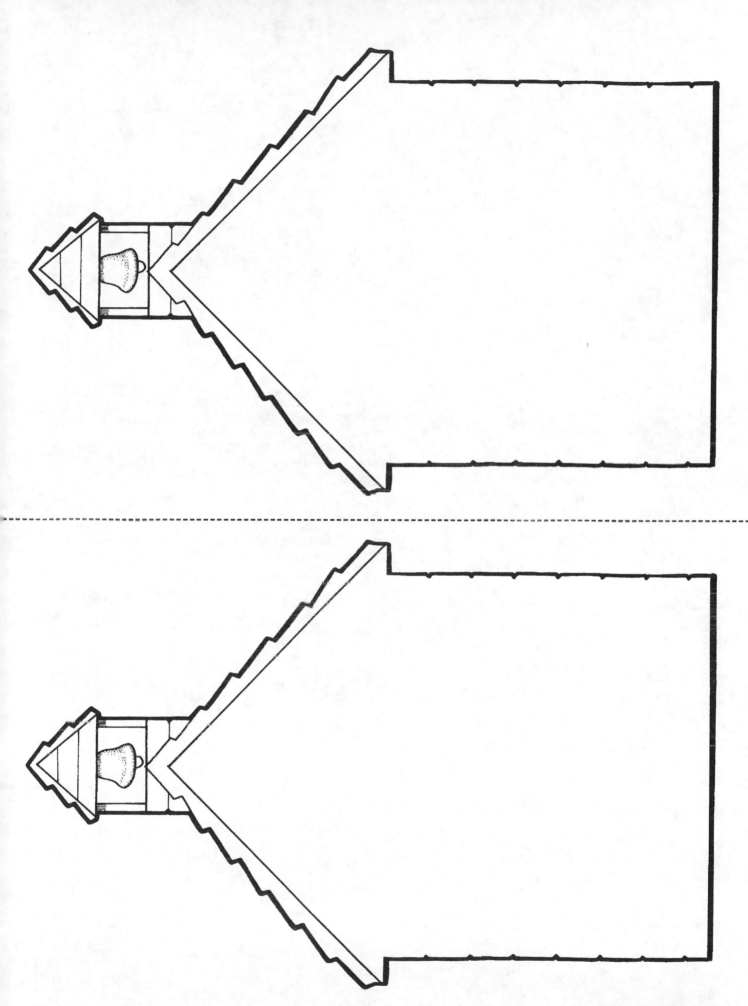

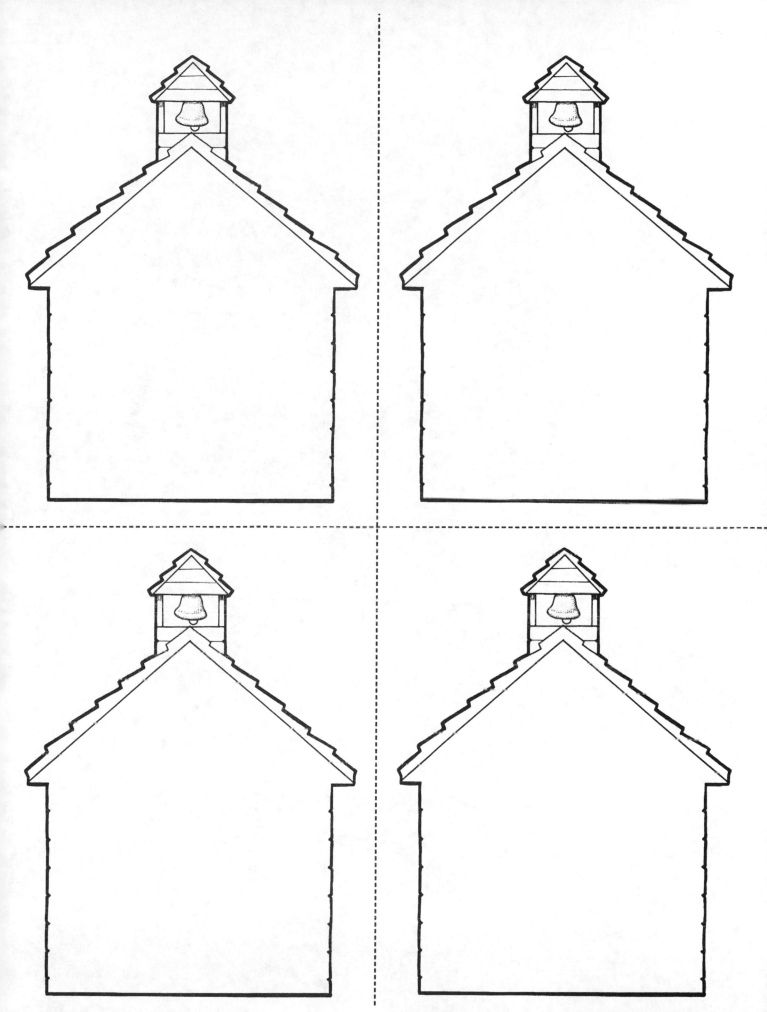

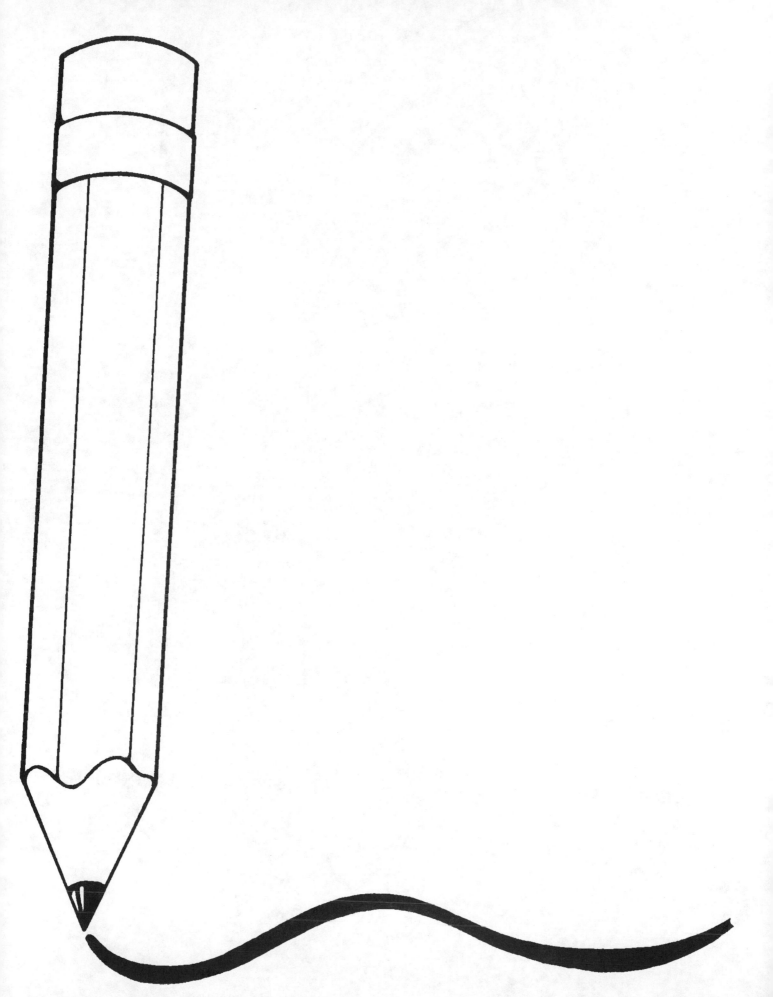

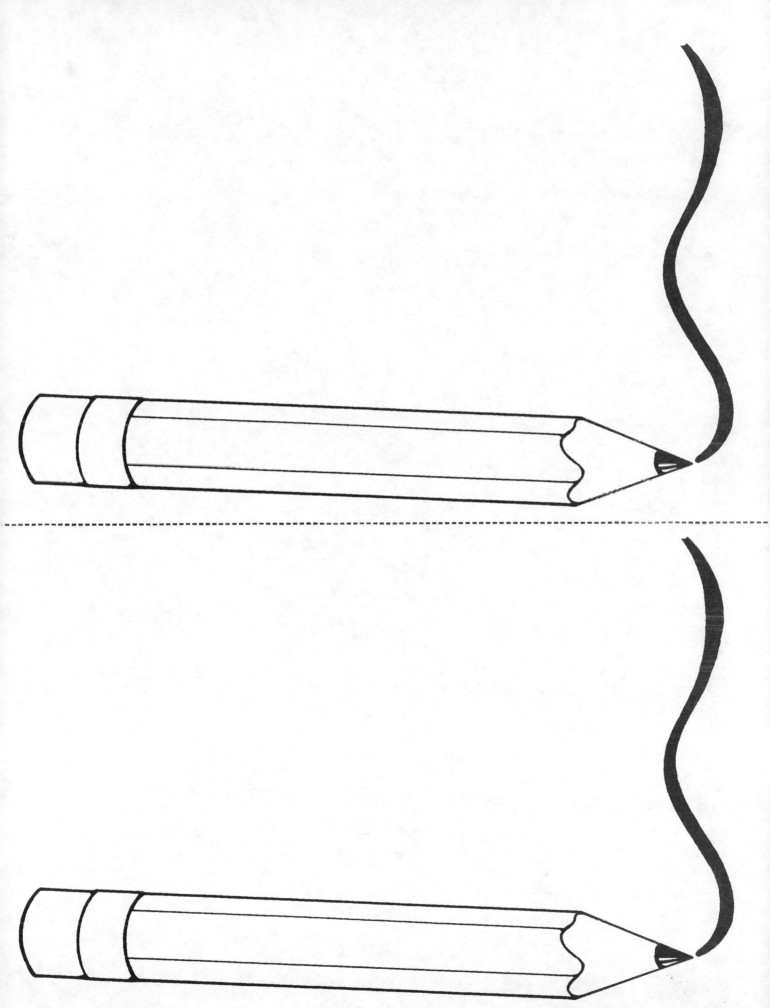

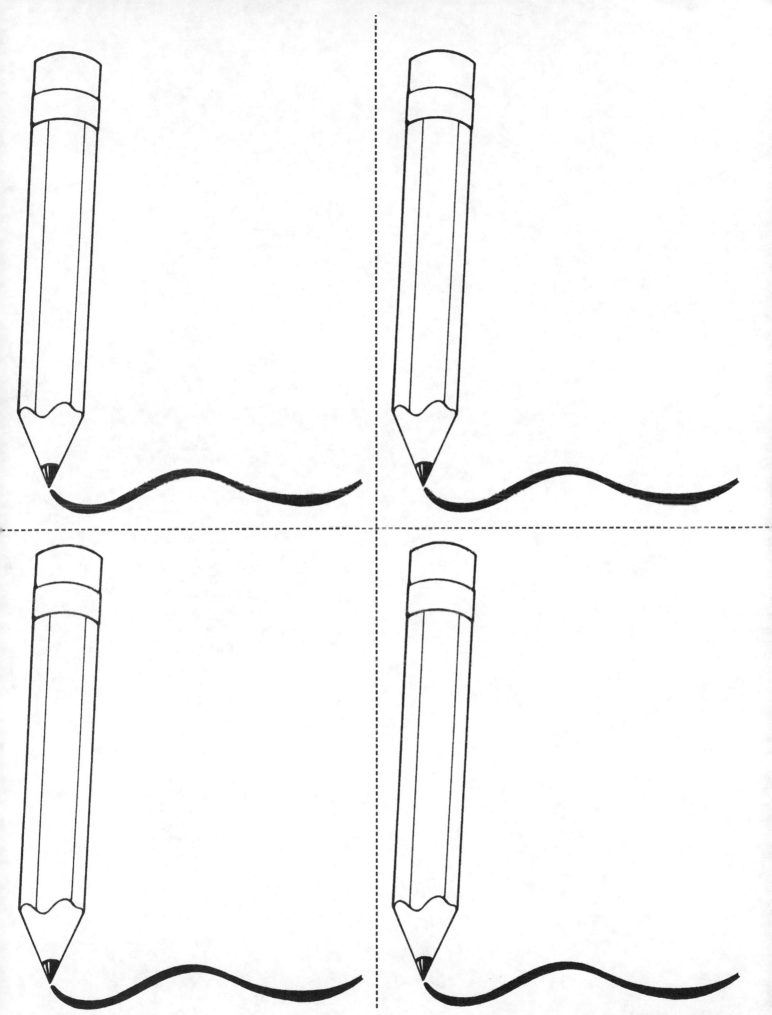

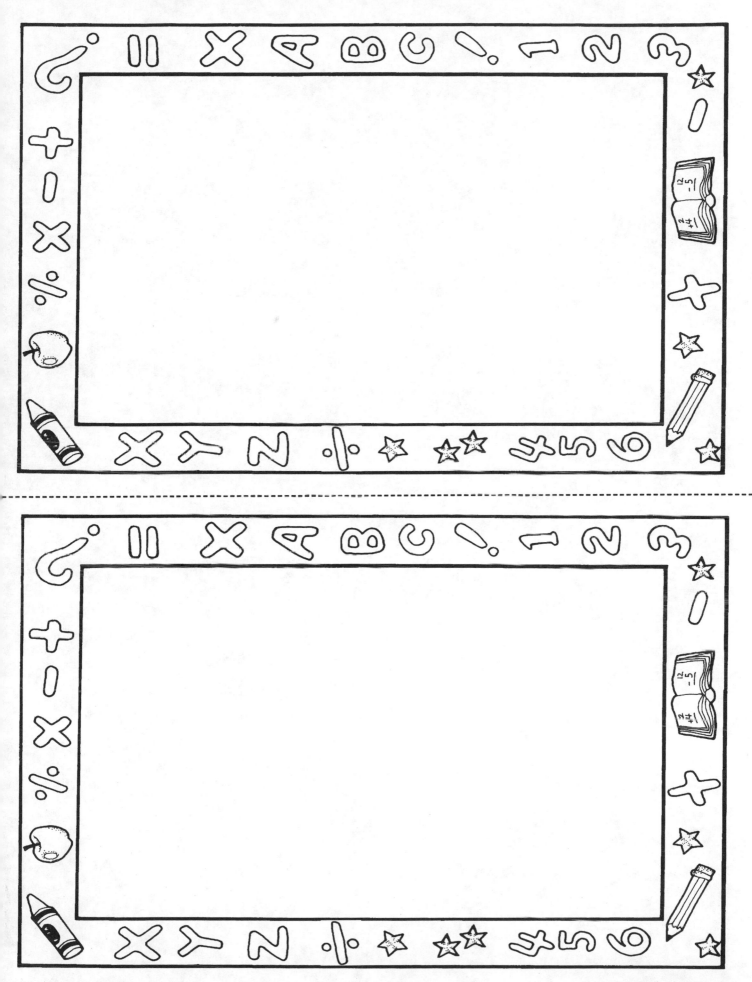

#2092 Jumbo Borders Book

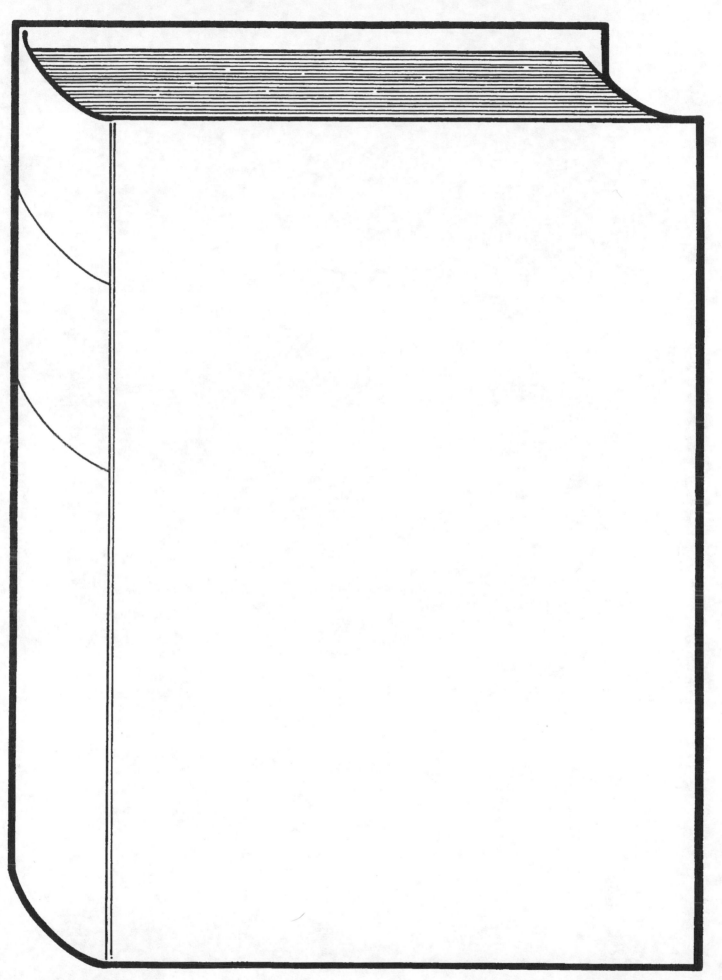

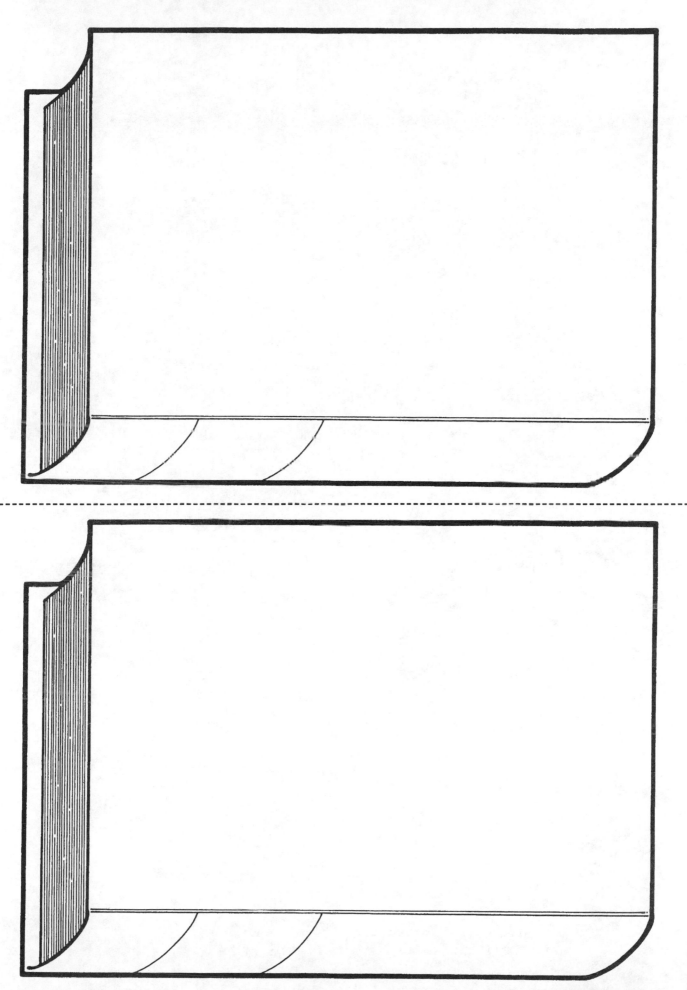

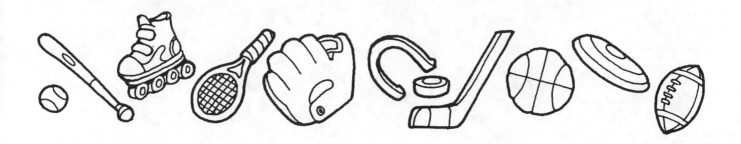

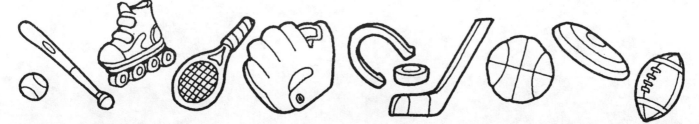

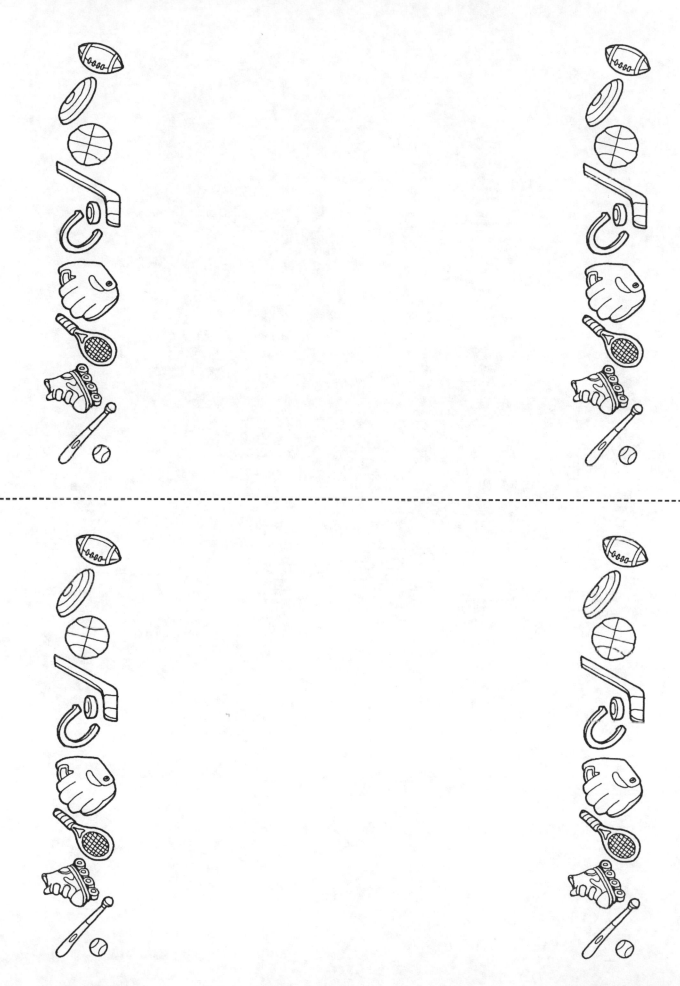

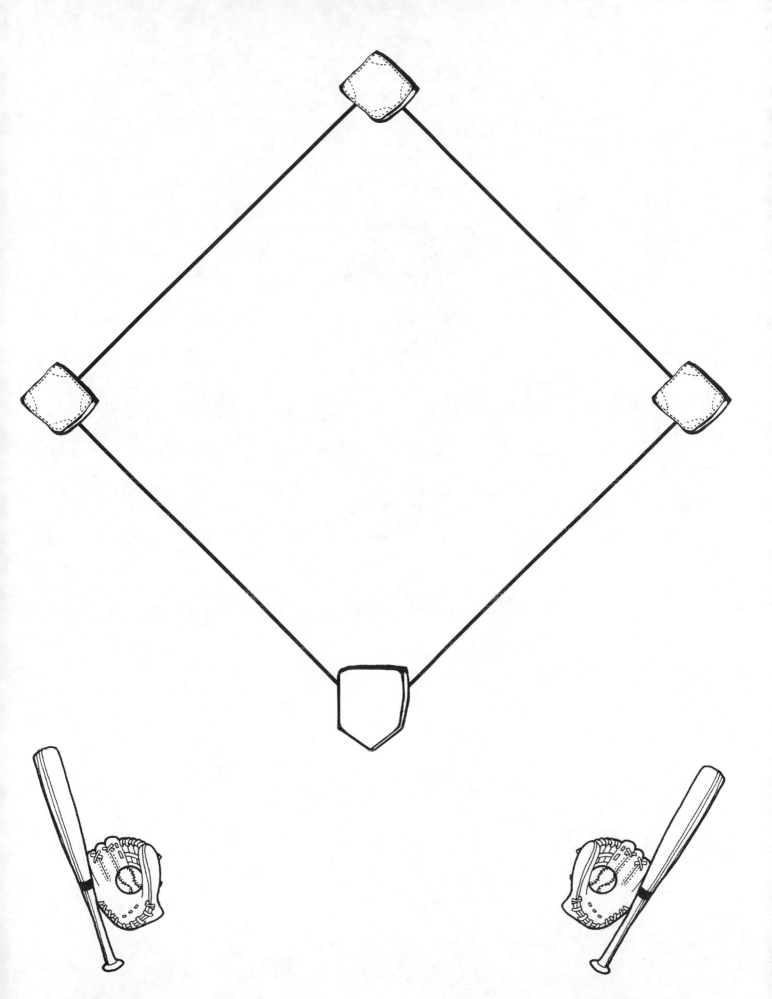

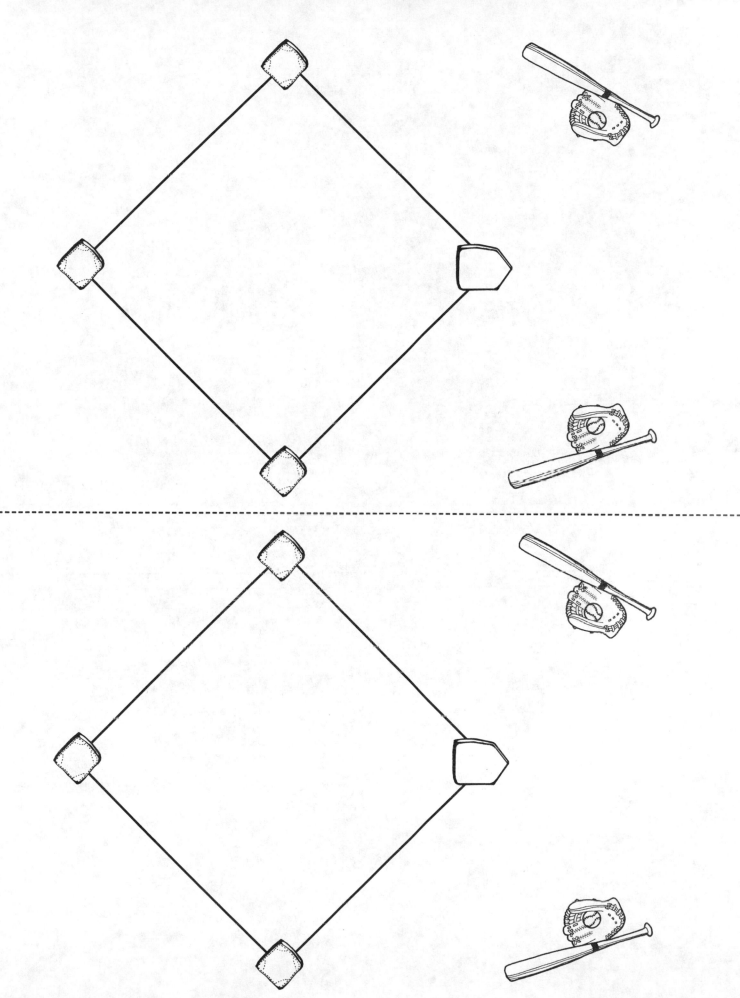

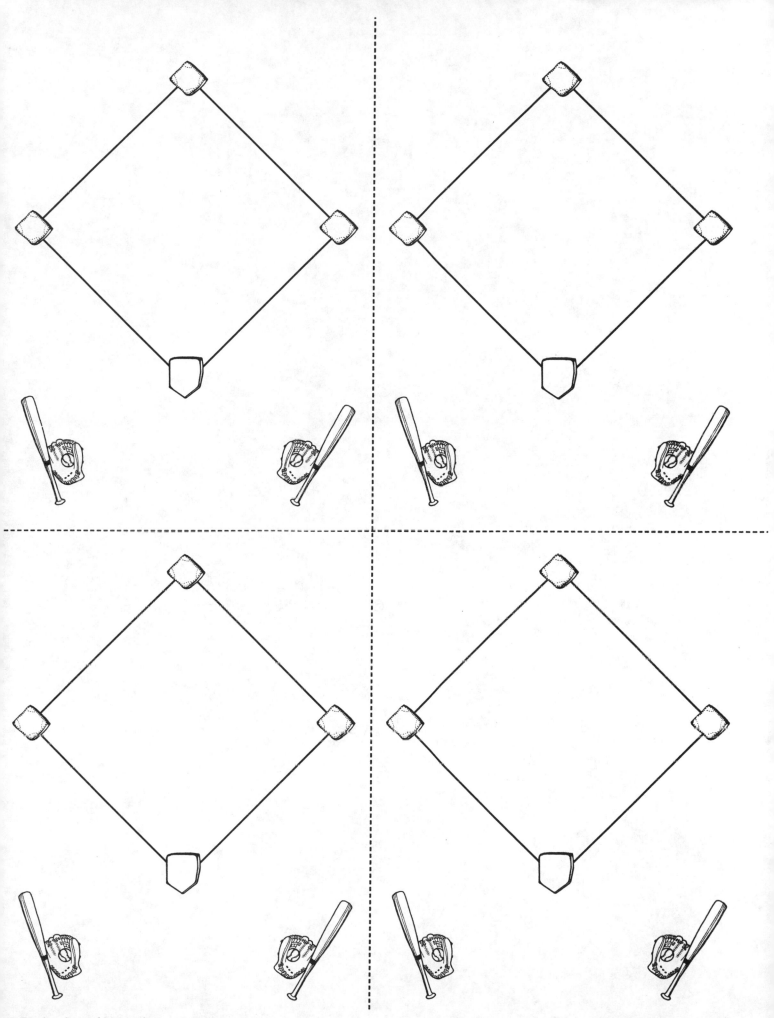

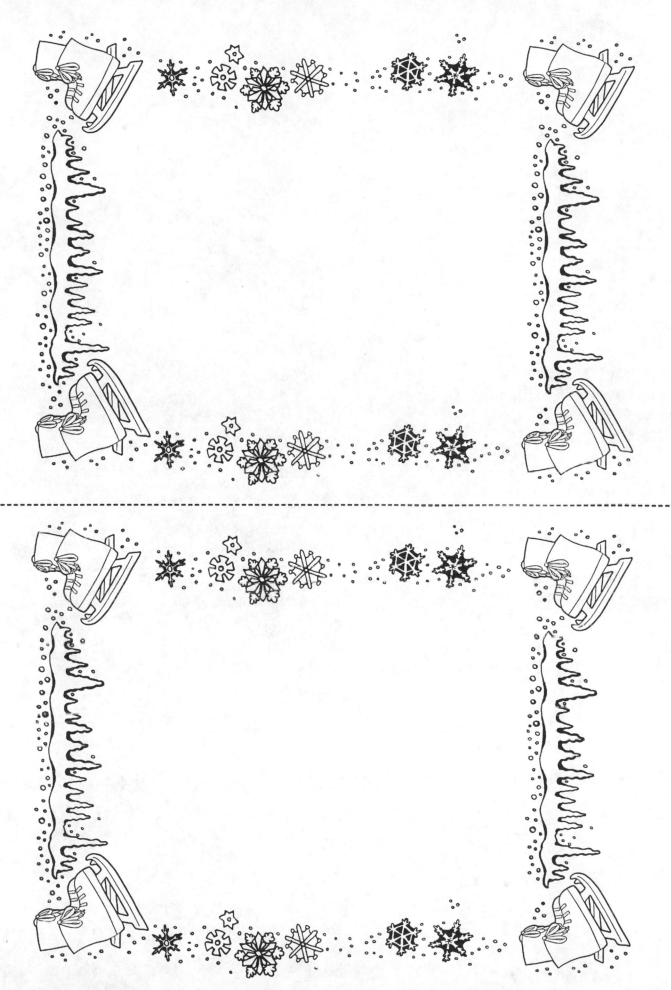